**WORSHIP RESOURCES FOR
THE SUNDAY SERVICE**

James F. Weekley

PRAISE AND THANKSGIVING

6810 / ISBN 0-89536-792-0

This volume is dedicated in honor of my mother,

Helen Hanson Weekley

whose enthusiasm for living

has made my understanding of God clearer.

Prayer: Our Last Survival Kit?

"Many people are so overwhelmed by what they think is wrong with them that they cannot see what they have going for them."

— *Bob Hope*

The energy crisis with which we are struggling has taught us at least one lesson: solar energy is where it's at. The future destiny of our economy lies not in the ground, but in the heavens. The potential is there. It's just a matter of creating the right technology.

Our lengthy debate over the proper function of worship, following Vatican II, has gleaned a similar truth. Personal and congregational renewal will happen only when its power is extracted from THE SON. Our destiny as God's people does not rest in the ground with an occupied tomb, but in the vastness of God's Spirit. ". . . seek the things that are above, where Christ is." (Colossians 3:1)

Yet, in spite of the serious attention we have given to the dynamics of worship over the past decade, for most denominations worship attendance continues to plummet. There has to be an attributing factor somewhere. Like solar energy, the potential is there. Could the problem converge upon our failure to follow through the disciplines of prayer? Somehow we must (a) regain our people's attention (Pac Man and cable TV haven't helped), and (b) articulate a need for spiritual renewal and committed follow-through.

In this volume we will attempt to focus on the specifics of prayer. What are the concrete problems we are facing? What do we hope to accomplish for the world through our prayers? It is hoped that the ecumenical language for the near-future church will be prayer. By concentrating our prayer frequencies on real need-struggling issues, the prodigal child will see that the church is worth returning to. The jubilant feast of renewal awaits!

— James Weekley

Table of Contents

1. THE NEW YEAR

Invocation
Our Timeless Spirit, who moves history with redemptive purpose, be present in our gathering today. You have come as our Friend many times before. We were warmed in your presence. Rekindle, again, that experience as we enter your hallowed presence. Amen

The Prayer of Confession
Our Father of time, that opportunity is golden again. The year before us brims with exploding possibilities. We should feel totally excited . . . yet . . . the sensation of guilt keeps seeping back before us. The opportunities of __(date)__ remain tarnished by our indecisiveness and complacency. Why do we seek to plow a new field when the adjoining one stands unharvested? Does this suggest that we have taken on too many projects which we cannot handle adequately?

Father, forgive our negligence in passing off, too quickly, hindsight for foresight, unseasoned knowledge for the whole truth. Help us to grow from our blunders of the past and to redefine our narrow view of the future. Most importantly, may we respond to your grace with a grasp of new beginnings, with renewed joy and with a determination to be ourselves for a change. Amen

The Prayer of Intercession
Our Father of time and eternity, who gives stability to a rapidly changing society, we acknowledge those who have become victims of change. Through predetermined circumstances, each day becomes an uphill struggle.They find it difficult to hold up under the daily strain of living.

For some, time becomes not an asset or a gift for opportunity, but a hurdle. It may be a despised job . . . even a sour marriage. *Challenge their thinking so they may begin to reorder their priorities.*

We acknowledge parents who are unable to cope with new responsibilities thrust upon them. A new child brings additional financial strain. *Help them to cultivate patience and to discover that the most beautiful things in life are worth waiting for.*

And, to those whose complacency is challenged by new ideas and innovative approaches to living — perhaps enrolling in college

after age forty — meet their need to excel. *Open them to the joys of discovery and the anticipation of growth possibilities.*
You provided your followers with a new burst of power when you said:
THE LORD'S PRAYER

Offertory Sentences
1 Chronicles 16:29

Offertory Prayer
The outpouring of your blessings are as countless as the galaxies. In these days of new beginnings and with these gifts, we wish to thank you. Amen

The Prayer Before the Homily
During this transitional period we experience mixed emotions. We seek a clearer direction — one which will unscramble our confusion. Your word is changeless. Give us the grace to live with that in these days. Amen

The Dismissal/Benediction
Our eternal Father, sustain us today with the courage to accept change, the ability to accept it without too much complaint, and the patience to accept our mistakes — because many of them will be repeated again. Amen

2. CHRISTIAN FELLOWSHIP

Invocation

Father, what can we expect from this encounter with you today? It is our hope that we will gain strength from our communion with each other. May we also learn to walk on knees that have been tried with the fires of confession and renewal. Amen

The Prayer of Confession

Lord, how frequently we conceive you in images, instead of experiences. We create a plastic Jesus — not a personal Friend; a stained glass Savior — not a living mystery; a Victorian creed — not a living organism. We are threatened by the closeness of your presence and the nearness of our neighbors. Lord, when are we going to get our fellowship act together? Where would we be without each other?

We are tired of 'being' without 'living.' We are lonely because we deliberately cut off wholesome opportunities to be with others. Tighten now the bonds of our sensitive care for each other. Heighten our awareness that you are no farther away than a silent prayer. Like a river, flow through us with your amazing grace. Amen

The Prayer of Intercession

O God, we remember the answer from the Puritan catechism which asked, "What is the purpose of life? To love God and to enjoy him forever." Doesn't that mean you made us primarily to fellowship with you? If so, then what is happening to our society? What is happening to people whose daily life-pattern has become cold, insensitive, and impersonal?

O God, we agonize with their struggle. They feel unloved and unacceptable. To compensate, they fabricate walls to cut off warm intimacy; they dig cellars to avoid honest confrontation; they construct attics to be world spectators. *Forgive them — and us — for failing to become active participants in your fellowship. Help us to take our church school classes and informal gatherings more seriously.*

We also focus upon those who would fellowship with us if only good health and distance would permit, those confined to convalescent homes and military bases. *For them we call upon your grace*

12

for assurance to remind them that there are friends who still care.
Accept us with the warmth of your presence as we share in your Son's Prayer:
THE LORD'S PRAYER

Offertory Sentences
Galatians 6:10

The Offertory Prayer
We who are so fortunate, Father, experience the grace of acceptance. Receive now these tokens of compassion. May they bring renewed joy to those who live in darkness. Amen

The Prayer of Homily
Like little children listening to a master storyteller, we gather around your Word. Speak words of wisdom to our simple minds, and words of comfort to our weak and heavy-laden hearts. Amen

The Dismissal/Benediction
Leader: Go forth into the light of God's awakening presence to declare his generous promises.
People: We respond to his new challenge.
Leader: Haven't you made a similar pledge before?
People: Yes, but at this time we find ourselves a year older and, we hope, wiser. God's grace will equip us for the task ahead. Amen

3. CHRISTIAN TRUTH

Invocation
Lord of ancient proverbs and contemporary truths, who gives the wise a deeper insight into the uncertainties of life, we come with uplifted hearts . . . in praise. Cleanse our thoughts of half-truths. Reinforce our courage with a grit that knows no compromise. Amen

The Prayer of Confession
In a mad dash, many of us approach truth like opening a can of alphabet soup — hoping to scramble together some magical formula for renewal. From false truths which wheel-and-deal without integrity; from pious truths which comfort without pain; from programmed truths which give us only what we want to hear, DELIVER US.

Father, when will it dawn upon us that truth comes only after peace and justice have been achieved? Today we are seeing that knowledge is not the final answer to our complicated problems. Somewhere amid the struggle to be our authentic selves and to liberate the oppressed, truth will be reborn. Through the unity of your grace, Father, heal us with that assurance. Amen

The Prayer of Intercession
Lord of justice and mercy, a cry goes forth from our land. Each moment that passes disease, hunger, and political exploitation take their toll. From collapsing bedroom walls, the cry of infant children scream for an embrace, a gesture of love, anything. Do we want to hear? *Lord, rattle our complacency. With our ballot, may we push for more adequate housing and parental care.*

From the marble-enclosed walls of state legislature, the rhetoric of equal rights for physically and sexually-abused children is offered . . . but somehow the buck continues to be passed. What has happened to our zeal for protest? *Lord, turn us inside out. May their hope for deliverance become our crusade for justice.*

From the windowless brick walls of the factory, the bitter complaint of the worker being paid less than minimum wage is voiced. Do we pretend to care only for our comfortable home and well-nourished children? *Lord, grant us the courage to be your mouthpiece of truth through our purchasing and write-our-congressperson power.*

Lord, hear our prayer for the oppressed and the forgotten on every continent. They are many in number, but their cause is one. Through the combined miracle of faith and grace, may they become less desperate and more hopeful for your never-failing promises.

Centuries ago you planted that seed in the hearts of your own when you prayed:
THE LORD'S PRAYER

Offertory Sentences
Luke 12:48

The Offertory Prayer
Lord, how shall the world experience spiritual liberation without a knowledge of your truth? As we participate in this sharing effort, may we help to contribute to the possibilities of a brighter hope. Amen

The Prayer Before The Homily
Lord, descend upon us as freshly fallen dew. With a Word which calms and tranquilizes, cool our anxieties and reinforce our strained relationships. Only then can we inch closer to personal happiness and world peace. Amen

The Dismissal/Benediction
Lord, together we have shared as a covenant people. Now, we depart to practice the miracle of your heart-transforming love. Watch over us until we return here next week. Amen

4. HUMAN RELATIONS DAY

Invocation

There are storm clouds on our horizons, Lord. That darkness has created prejudice and hatred in our relationships. We have fled to this sanctuary for another glimpse of your pure light. Having opened to us the floodgates of your throne of grace, may we become better neighbors to the lonely, friendlier to strangers, and easier to live with at home. Amen

The Prayer of Confession

"Where's the magic?" we ask. Are we not here to cash in on simple solutions . . . those carefully reasoned plans of action? We strive for a saner world and a cleaner environment. Yet, why do we speak out for human decency only in the company of cushioned pews and well-wishers? Why do we tolerate racial and ethnic references as cute and natural? Why are we reluctant to challenge the world of poverty and oppression? Could it be that we have failed to master the spiritual world within?

Forgive us for being *what* we are. Through the mystery of grace remind us *whose* we are . . . yours! Within the commitment of caring and reaching, direct us to *where* we should be. Amen

The Prayer of Intercession

God of new beginnings and thundering truth, who has called each of us to participate in a global community, our planet has become smaller. The communications revolution has seen to that. Also, it has become more complicated. How well you can see that by our actions. Many among our human family witness daily the slow erosion of their rights by powers greater than their comprehension . . . their living space has become increasingly restricted by government red tape and insensitivity. O God, they are short on hope. They have long ago abandoned their most cherished dreams. Where is their deliverer?

O God, don't you see the Smiths, recently retired, who with a $350 monthly pension must make a choice between fifty gallons of fuel oil for their heater and a sufficient protein diet until the next check comes.

Don't you see the Thompsons, whose small farm has been

rezoned for industrial use — without their consent? Don't you see the Cabanas, a migrant family, who never spend Christmas and Easter in the same house?

O God, if ever someone's need qualified for your justice, surely it must be theirs! They are listening and hoping. They are not asking for a miracle — just an even chance to begin at least one day in their lives on ground level. O God, we are listening, too. Summon us, your covenant people, to that task of righteous healing. We want to become a part of this new beginning. We possess the faith, the gifts, and the resources. What are we waiting for?

THE LORD'S PRAYER

Offertory Sentences
1 Peter 1:22

The Offertory Prayer
We pray, our Father, that the dedication of these offerings will not only symbolize our love for you, but also our commitment to all those in need of acceptance and friendship. Amen

The Prayer Before the Homily
As we break ground on a new day with unlimited possibilities, remind us of the brokenness of humankind. Sensitize us to their needs as we break together your Bread of Life. Amen

The Dismissal/Benediction
Leader: Go now as a liberated people. Try your new wings. As a song with a voice, share your exploding joy.
People: We will cease from cursing the dãrkness. We will rejoice in his light. We are a new people with purpose.
Leader: What will you do with your freedom? Where will you chart your course?
People: We are free to invest in the hopes of tomorrow. Like Jacob, God's blessing will go with us. Amen

5. SCIENCE AND RELIGION

Invocation
In spite of our preoccupation with technological achievements, we desire to be assured that you are not too far from us. In this hour of praise and renewal, come to challenge us in the laboratory of our minds — as well as in the sanctuary of our hearts. Amen

The Prayer of Confession
Infinite Creator, you have said, "I am the light of the world." We say, "Better things for better living through chemistry." You have said, "I am the Way." We say, "I'm OK, you're OK, as long as we can retain our arsenals of war." You have said, "I am the Good Shepherd." We say, "Twinkle, twinkle, my computer superstar, I need not wonder what you are."

We pray not only for forgiveness. We ask that you will challenge our shrines of technology. Give us the wisdom to ask the right questions, and the common sense to be selective with the answers that meet real needs. Heal our aloneness. Sustain us with the assurance that our lives are not equations to be mastered, but delicate creations to be loved. Amen

The Prayer of Intercession
Lord, before we applaud too quickly our technological advancements — laser surgery, the development of artificial limbs, projected orbiting solar labs, caution us to consider the timeless words of Winston Churchill: "We have not journeyed all this way across the centuries, across the oceans, across the mountains, across the prairies, because we are made of suger candy."

Our sustaining power, both for ourselves and as nations, had its source in your truth. It is when we make advancements without foresight and fabricate mechanical novelties void of humane ends, that we get into trouble. Lord, when that happens, some of us, having lost touch with you, are incapable of seeking and finding you.

Hear us now, Lord, as we speak on their behalf. We see a hospital nurse who in one day administers pain-relieving drugs to a post-surgical patient, and agonizes later when she must "keep alive" an unconscious elderly man whose mind is permanently impaired. *Please, Lord, communicate your will to her.*

We see a young medical student who must soon choose between a lucrative practice and a need-fulfilling service in a rural community. *Impress upon her the fact that narrow loyalties often bring a locked-in loneliness before age forty.*

Lord, spare each of us an early grave. Remind us anew that unselfish giving translates into hopeful-and-upward living.

Your prayer for the abundant and resourceful life, potentially, moves us into that venture:

THE LORD'S PRAYER

Offertory Sentences
2 Corinthians 8:7

Offertory Prayer
Help us to remember, dear Lord, that successful living involves far more than a knowledge of computer programming and chemical formulas. Rather, it is through our voluntary sharing that genuine progress takes place in our world. Amen

The Prayer Before the Homily
Your gospel of peace is also a gospel of sanity. Convict us with a new honesty about where we are going with our technology. Energize us with the truth that progress without growth is chaos without hope. Amen

The Dismissal/Benediction
Now, as you return to your little corner of the world, go with the taste of a new challenge. Be a possibility people. Transform the knowledge of that world with lasting peace and wisdom. Amen

DIVINE PROVIDENCE

Invocation

Our Father and Creator, who is more powerful than galactic black holes, yet whose love is as warm as a mother's embrace, infiltrate anew our broken hopes. Assure us that you are with us always . . . now . . . tomorrow . . . forever . . . Amen

The Prayer of Confession

Our Cosmic Light, your magnificent presence floods upon us. As it sparked those first life-beginning molecules on the face of the waters, it solicits from us new creations and beginnings. But, its warmth threatens our ice insensitivity. It resurrects the beast of primeval fear which we have allowed to grow out of control. Its light becomes so blinding that we seek shelter within the shadows of our prejudices. Our amoeba-like faith has allowed the cancer cells of pride to eat into our potential for self-realization and growth.

Explode, we pray, the myths we have created in the name of progress. Now, more than ever, grant us a more fulfilling acceptance within your grace and within the fellowship of our church community. May you become so great a Force in our lives that even doubt and depression will become past history. Amen

The Prayer of Intercession

God of Joshua, Jeremiah, and Jesus, your power comes to rekindle our burned-out hope; your grace comes to rebuild us from the debris of our failures; your love, the flesh and bones of that grace, comes to reverse our prejudices with trust.

Not all persons acknowledge that power as the vital pulse beat of their lives. Frustrated by a complex society they cannot handle, they lash out in anger against you. *Please teach them that honesty speaks louder than an unexamined hand-me-down faith.*

There are many of our youth who call the hand of the church by asking, "Why do you have so many expensive conferences while people are starving by the millions?" *Remind them that truth is launched when we begin asking the right kind of questions.*

There is a native American family who has been deprived of fifty acres of ranchland by the red tape of government. *Spare them from bitterness. Enable them to see that love speaks louder than violence.*

With the vastness of your heavenly power, etch your will into the minds and hearts of all who feel unloved and unwanted. Draw them into your church family where genuine acceptance awaits.

Let us affirm the security of that acceptance in these — your words: THE LORD'S PRAYER

Offertory Sentences
Ephesians 1:14

Offertory Prayer
Almighty God, as we cast our devotion before your throne of grace, accept us in the present tense; also, accept our gifts for the day-by-day work of your kingdom. Amen

The Prayer Before the Homily
O God, whose vastness is incomprehensible, our faith, as a dormant seed, awaits your nourishing strength. In the outpouring of your truth, transform our thinking into action. Then we can continue to grow and to live with purpose. Amen

The Dismissal/Benediction
May the Lord our God be with us, as he was with our fathers; may he never forsake us. May he give us the desire to do his will in everything, and to obey all the commandments and instructions he has given our ancestors. Amen (Paraphrase of 1 Kings 8:57-58)

7. CHRISTIAN LOVE

Invocation
Dear Lord, who has given us faith and the eyes of hope, challenge us to live and worship with an active heart of love. Amen

The Prayer of Confession
O God, we want to be more loving than we are; but we find it difficult to relate to the unlovely and the unloved. We want to be transformed into butterflies of hope, but our cocoons of self-centeredness keep us locked in. We want to address the needs of the hungry and the unemployed, but are easily turned off by their apathy to help themselves. We want to accept your forgiveness, but only if it applies to our minor league sins.

Show us not what we *want* for others, but what we *need* to do in the name of your Son. With the gentle touch of your grace, anoint us with a truth that is forever beginning and a compassion that won't quit. Amen

The Prayer of Intercession
God of infinite compassion and patience, you have instructed us, through your Son, that perfect love can be disclosed through us. It is so grace-full that fear and prejudice can be dispelled.

Yet, we must ask, "Why haven't some responded favorably to that potential for their lives?" We summon your acceptance, O God, for those who have not shared fully in your love.

We pray for parents who scream impatiently at their children. *Help them understand that you have given them the responsibility of molding their character.*

We pray for those who babble in tongues of twisted gossip. *May we confront them openly and honestly with the words, "Friend, are you certain that's true?"*

We pray for those who rarely say anything positive about others. We know they desperately need a friend for acceptance. *May we become an advocate of your love to them.*

Your acceptance is spiritual wholeness. It can heal the vastness — every cell of our being. Why must we be oblivious to that beautiful and flowering possibility? Why do we insist upon protecting ourselves from that intimacy?

Work now your love through our hands and feet as we gain inspiration from these words:
THE LORD'S PRAYER

Offertory Sentences
Romans 14:12

Offertory Prayer
We thank you, Father, for your daily blessings of health, fresh air, and family relationships. With these tokens of love may we see that it is only through giving that we lose ourselves in service to others. Amen

The Prayer Before the Homily
Your love-as-truth opens us to the possibilities of a better world. We see violence . . . war . . . hunger — all testimonies of our ignorance. Does it make any sense to live that way? Love is the only answer, the only way. What are we waiting for? Amen

The Dismissal/Benediction
God's love is not passive. And, it is the only ingredient capable of giving us coping power. As you wrestle with what it means to be human, be assured that his Force will direct you. Amen

8. THE FIRST SUNDAY IN LENT

Invocation
The long and difficult road to the cross rises before us. We begin as pilgrims. We pray that you will give us the grace to sharpen our conscience and the wisdom to lengthen our patience. Amen

The Prayer of Confession
Leader: Lord, as Lent begins we are, once more, ready to move into those pre-Easter spiritual gymnastics. But what are we trying to prove . . . that our faith is capable of flexing its muscles if it has to?
People: We ask, "What road will we travel?" We know that the long and narrow road will require commitment and sacrifice.
Leader: Lord, won't this require deep soul-searching? Will we be so busy with school and community activities that we won't have the time to reevaluate who we really are . . . and how we might be open to the suffering needs of others?
People: We will begin our journey this morning with the assurance that your manna of love will nourish us by day and the light of your peace will sustain us by night. Amen

The Prayer of Intercession
Lord, most of the time we conceive your residence somewhere 'out there' among the vast regions of outer space. On the other hand, isn't your presence to be found within the minute space of our minds?

Lord, this Lenten encounter calls us to draw deeply from those inner reserves. Without those living waters, the capacity for vision and hope subside. Why, then, are the springs often so dry and taste-less? For those who have not experienced you as the Master Potter of human destiny, how much greater is their need. As our physical hearts are no more than a beat from your eternity, so our spiritual hearts are no more than a simple prayer away from your presence.

Lord, in humility, we summon your Spirit to our points of weak-ness and to the needs of special persons:

. . . An unemployed father caught in the inflation trap, with barely enough money to meet a monthly mortgage on their home;

. . . A runaway youth who sought acceptance at home, but wan-dered elsewhere to find it with a pimp or a pusher;

. . . An imprisoned homemaker who feels she's someone special, but has no one with whom to share her dreams.

Lord, identify with us in our Lenten-faith struggle. Give us the eyes of eagles so that we may keep sight of your love in all circumstances. May our eyes radiate forth that truth as we pray:
THE LORD'S PRAYER

Offertory Sentences
Ephesians 5:2

Offertory Prayer
Our Messiah and King, forgive our indifference to the challenge of your cross. With these offerings may we ready ourselves — our minds, souls, and bodies — for the triumphant joy of the resurrection. Amen

The Prayer Before the Homily
Father, we have difficulty in attempting to discover who you are because we do not know who we are. May Lent be a time for asking the right kind of questions. May your Word open us to that new venture as we immerse ourselves in your Gospel of proclamation. Amen

The Dismissal/Benediction
Leader: The path to the cross will not always be so clear. Detours and U-turns will lure you. At times you will wonder why you are traveling that way in the first place.
People: Nonetheless, we have to go forward and upward. We have been called to fulfill a specific mission: to grow and to serve.
Leader: You are saying that nothing will be able to separate you from that conviction.
People: Yes, our voice will be praise and our language will be truth. Amen

9. THE SECOND SUNDAY IN LENT

Invocation
Like the petals of an unfolding flower, we lift up our hearts in praise, Father, grateful that we are with you again. Having refreshed ourselves in your presence, may our priorities become less confusing and our goals more realistic. Amen

The Prayer of Confession
As you called Lazarus from the tomb, from the dark shadows of fear and insecurity, we emerge cautiously. We are reluctant to present our real selves in complete openness. When your light summons us, we respond, but remain dead to the feelings of those closest to us. You have called us to roll aside the stone of greed, that obsession which seeks to own us, and we find our courage lacking. Thunder upon us, we pray, your mandate for renewal, so that we will never retreat into the cryptic darkness of apathy. Empower us with your Spirit so nothing will ever draw us from your power. Amen

The Prayer of Intercession
We journey into the second phase of our Lenten experience. We have not arrived by any means. We still feel restless like Adam stumbling through the thistle east of Eden. If that were not enough, there are those persistent dragons of doubt and impatience, lurking, ready to meet us. Father, why is there such a restlessness, much like spring fever, that arises to repel our call to the new life? Father, we do not request a formula for instant perfection. We simply want to be better than we are. We, also, petition on behalf of those persons who might find their daily struggles more tolerable:
. . . Those who complain because they must 'give up' desserts for Lent, yet rarely consider the millions who do not have adequate bread and vegetables;
. . . Media advertisers who exploit sexual weakness and models who will sell their bodies to the highest bidder;
. . . A pregnant woman who is oblivious to the effect of her alcohol consumption upon her unborn child.
Father, as you walked with Enoch, please walk behind us in the dawn, before us in the day, and enfold us with your arms in the dark

of the night. We affirm that acceptance in all our joys and struggles as we pray:
THE LORD'S PRAYER

Offertory Sentences
Luke 9:23

Offertory Prayer
O God, we ask that we will not only be cheerful givers to the One who gave himself for us, but that we will assume our responsibilities in sharing the demands of the cross. Amen

The Prayer Before the Homily
In this period of self-examination and confrontation, we know that does not excuse us from our participation in the struggles of the world. Measure us by your Word in order that we may assess where we are. Amen

The Dismissal/Benediction
Father, we go forth with a tougher resolve. We remember your promise of forgiving acceptance and inner renewal. Help us to match that with a commitment to the alleviation of hunger and exploitation. Amen

10. TEMPTATION

Invocation
Father, we pray, "Lead us not into temptation," while generally we allow ourselves to be taken there by others. In this worship confrontation enable us to recognize that you do have the power to "deliver us from evil."

The Prayer of Confession
Lord, our obsession to move too fast with too much has made us impatient. Even within the past decade our technology has given us increased power over life and death. We have not altogether cradled it responsibly. For some of us, power has corrupted. It has not sharpened our sensitivity to human need.

How shall we handle that overwhelming desire to meet our timetables? Lord, we strive for a new direction. In that task give us the common sense to say *yes* to your uncompromising Spirit. Then we will be in a better position to say *no* to the influences of the forces of darkness. Amen

The Prayer of Intercession
Lord Jesus, you acknowledge better than anyone how the power of temptation could seek to cloud one's spiritual perception. No one has ever been offered what the Prince of darkness tempted you with: all of the empires of the world. But you struck back by affirming the unyielding will of your Father. He is not subject to compromise.

We are, however, masters of compromise. We forget too easily the beauty of your love and the consequences of our sins. Unlike yourself, our capacity to resist is low. It is our concern that your Spirit will make us stronger in tempting circumstances . . . and do help us to avoid them in the first place. We request further that the delicate compassion of your grace will meet the needs of persons in crisis.

. . . One who steals materials daily from his or her job. Remind them that ". . . whatever a man sows, that he will also reap." (Galatians 6:7)

. . . Parents whose expensive recreational tastes omit family participation — hence robbing their children of family growth experiences. Remind them, ". . . bring them up with the loving discipline the Lord himself approves." (Paraphrase of Ephesians 6:4)

. . . Those who use the social benefits of the church to advance their business ends. Remind them, "Wherever your treasure is, there will your heart be also." (Luke 12:34)

Now, remind us of your redeeming power and forgiveness with these beautiful words:
THE LORD'S PRAYER

Offertory Sentences
Psalm 66:13-14

Offertory Prayer
As we occupy ourselves with the self-giving work in your kingdom, Father, strengthen us. So empower us that, when temptation comes, we will be equipped to cope with it. Amen

The Prayer Before the Homily
Lord, our big problem, the shadow which consistently stands over us, is the Goliath of temptation. We want to practice that truth, but something tries to pull at us to do otherwise. Energize us with that living Word. Help us to stand firm when that force does come. Amen

The Dismissal/Benediction
The world awaits your witness. Overcome evil with goodness, gentleness, and self-control. Be hopeful and joyful. It's still God's world. Trust him and he will make things happen through you. Amen

11. PASSION SUNDAY

Invocation

The towering cross, with its timeless splinters and nails, stands, unmovable before us. We see that it isn't a hurdle to our faith but a passage — the only gateway to Easter hope. May we move that door ever more open in our worship experience this day. Amen

The Prayer of Confession

Dear God, who came with accepting love, yet who died in rejection, we shamefully admit that we have denied your healing power to others. We have made faith an aspirin tablet, joy a soap opera, hope an all-expense-paid-week-end fantasy island.

Why must we be so consumed by our insensitivity to human suffering and our moral indecisiveness? Why can't we reflect more intimately your love in our daily relationships?

Forgive our lack of trust, dear God. Stir us with an urgency to become more committed to those causes that outlast death itself. Opportunities for witness come quickly. Equip us with grit and readiness. Amen

The Prayer of Intercession

How naive we are about your truth. We think being a Christian is easy — no blisters, no skinned knees — clean, immaculate, neat. You found that a welcome mat was not laid before you in every town on your itinerary.

Then when they discovered that your message spelled tough sacrifice and third-gear commitment, they became uneasy — often hostile. You did not back down, however. Your dedication was one-tracked, immovable. You even died for what you believed. Of course, Lord, few of us are willing to go that far. Does that mean we are any less committed? Do you still allow limping disciples to play in your league? We need your strength in our weakness. We need your power in our failures. We need your understanding because we know that you have walked in our shoes. Others desperately need you, too.

. . . Political and religious prisoners who defied exploitation in quest for justice.

. . . Elderly 'shut-ins' who cannot understand why church families will not visit them.

. . . A high school student deeply involved in peddling cocaine and doesn't know how to get out before it's too late.

Lord, help us to rejoice when our trials become too overbearing. Place before us — so that we may be sustained by them — memories of past joys and warm relationships. Assure us of their reoccurrence when you remind us of your response to suffering: THE LORD'S PRAYER

Offertory Sentences
John 15:13

Offertory Prayer
Teach us, our Father, that only in the sharing of the sufferings of other persons, will your Spirit open us to the opportunities for renewal and growth. Amen

The Prayer Before the Homily
Your Word exposes us to mental and physical adversity because it challenges the codes of the secular world. The "good news" suggests that the "old news" is inadequate. Grant us the vision never to lose sight of that. Amen

The Dismissal/Benediction
Lord, spare us of our narrow-mindedness if we forget the masses of humankind who have no spokesperson. As you journey with us through the valley of the shadow, walk with them, too. May their thirst for justice become yours, as well. Amen

12. PALM SUNDAY

Invocation
This is a jubilee day. We wave palm branches and peace banners in your name. Yet caution us, Lord, that unless we are willing to enploy peace in all our relationsips, the parade will be forgotten. Prepare our faith for that risk today. Amen

The Prayer of Confession
The fanfare has begun. The spirit is right and our praise soars skyward. But why are we so edgy? We have witnessed the parade before. Is it that which follows the parade which disturbs us? It's that guilt again. It throws us face-to-face with our denials, our failed opportunities for compassion. It exposes us to the tombs of apathy we have created at the expense of human abuse and suffering.

As we meet you, Lord Jesus, greet us with eyes of forgiveness. Remind us that, in spite of our rejection, our failures, you still accept us as your own. With that assurance, may we rejoice in your love — and be thankful. Amen

The Prayer of Intercession
Our Lord and King, we are too busy to recognize your triumphant entry. With our stereo ear phones tuned to a fever pitch, how can we perceive it? And, when your drama has passed, we ask, "When does the ticker-tape parade begin?" Ideally, we believe in your ultimate triumph of good over evil, right over might, light over darkness. We applaud Matthew's words, "Behold, my servant whom I have chosen . . . I will put my Spirit upon him." (12:18) But, when it comes to applying your truth specifically, we often become hesitant and organize a study committee.

Lord, it is our petition that you will enable us to become more active advocates on behalf of the earth's little people, the helpless and the 'used':

. . . Parentless children who are exploited in porno movies at age ten. What kind of future will they have with sex void of love?

. . . Women, abused and battered by their husbands, who are trapped by a tenth grade education. What kind of future will they have unless they sprout wings of faith — and fly?!

Come to us, now, as fresh as a fragrant, spring breeze. Lift us

up with this flower of hope:
THE LORD'S PRAYER

Offertory Sentences
Psalm 4:5

Offertory Prayer
As the citizens of Jerusalem received you as Messiah and King, receive now these offerings for the kingdom they failed to recognize. Amen

The Prayer Before the Homily
You have been transformed from Shepherd into King. A parade always draws a crowd. But, apart from the glamor of a royal ride, does our allegiance match our excitement? If not, we ask that your truth will help us to get our priorities reshuffled. Amen

The Dismissal/Benediction
Leader: The King has made his grand entrance into your hearts. It's now history.
People: The triumphant parade has been uplifting. We rejoice that Jesus is King.
Leader: What kind of King will you make him? Remember, either he dominates you, or you are dominated by lesser loyalties.
People: We are prepared to pay the cost of that struggle. We do not want to betray him. He will empower us when the showdown comes. Amen

13. EASTER SUNDAY

Invocation

The trumpets of the resurrection resound with the timeless words, "come," "see," "go," "tell." Come, Lord Jesus, and fill us with your alive-today presence. Amen

The Prayer of Confession

Our eternal Christ, who came to rule the world, not with the fullness of secular power, but from an empty tomb, we confess our negligence to live in rhythm with that drumbeat. Also, for a second-handed doubt which voids growth-producing questioning; for a fear of dying which drains our potential for creative living; for our insensitivity to the subtle inquiries of strangers on our Emmaeus road to faith; for our failure to act, talk, and pray *resurrection* in all our affairs; for substituting the love of our children for sugar-coated confessions and stylish clothing; like Peter, we confess our shortsighted failings. As the Master Potter of humankind, regrind, sanctify, and remold us into your image of caring love. Amen

The Prayer of Intercession

Our Lord and our God, we sense a strangeness, much like the calm following a raging storm. All nature is fresh and alive, bursting with fragrant beauty. We know that something magnificent has taken place. The lilies before us declare victorious power and peace. Even the sun has taken on a new significance. We have struggled in the darkness for too long; your sunrise is vibrant and renewing. For us, the stone of sin and death has been removed. But for others, a barrier still stands in the way of your glorified presence. They have either lost — or never tasted — the fruits of your Spirit.

. . . We pray for new life for spouses who have sustained the loss of their mates this past year. *Resurrect their failing hopes with opportunities to meet new friends and to make their days more productive.*

. . . We pray for new life for Soviet leaders whom we generally regard as hopeless and godless. *Renew our confidence in the miracle of your love, that occasional prayer can in fact help right to triumph over wrong.*

. . . We pray for new life for racists and bigots of every race, whose deep wounds of hate scar potential friendships. *Rekindle the truth that it is better to light a candle than to curse the darkness.*

In these days of heightened fear of nuclear annihilation, we plead desperately for a deeper sanity and faith in human potential for enlightenment. Keep that hope ever before us as we recall these words of peace:
THE LORD'S PRAYER

Offertory Sentences
1 Corinthians 15:58

Offertory Prayer
Father, Easter is a symbol of the brevity of life. Flowers wither. Money tarnishes. All of life is terminated in its appropriate season. But it is your love we leave behind that will continue to last. May these offerings contribute to that task. Amen

The Prayer Before the Homily
Christ Jesus, we are receptive to the explosion of your Word. Like the tomb of Joseph, death cannot hold it down. It is alive with a power that will never cease. Amen

The Dismissal/Benediction
Lord, we go forth in peace because we have experienced you, our Peacemaker. Your peace is tranquility, one which the world has failed to grasp. It silences even death itself. And where there is assurance, resurrection-life thrives. Amen

14. PRAYER

Invocation
Our Father, as we journey into the inner space of our hearts, welcome us with the warmth of your presence. Also, remind us to lay aside all jealousies and anxieties. Amen

The Prayer of Confession
Father God, we have a communication problem — with you. For reasons we cannot adequately explain, we have lost touch. We have failed to remove those obstacles which obstruct you presence. First, there is *impatience,* which acts quickly out of a fear to face the real *us* and our potential for maturity. Next, there are those last minute *compromises,* which we think suggest that you do not really listen until the evenings, when you are resting. Then come the ghosts of *guilt* who constantly remind us that we are not one hundred percent forgiven.

Father, this also leaves us with our inability — our fear to face the issue of others suffering — and our apathy to do anything about it. As you speak to us in the language of love and forgiveness, remind us of the possibilities of prayer. You have so many gifts to share with us. Help us to take the time to discover them. Amen

The Prayer of Intercession
Father, we do not have to be clever to converse with you. We know that you are a Friend, one who wishes to be spoken to like anyone else. For a change, Father, we do not come before your presence asking for favors. Today, we simply wish to say "thank you."

. . . We are grateful for the simple prayers of little children that change the hearts and minds of complex adults.

. . . We are grateful for the agonizing prayers of the terminally ill cancer patient who continues to retain both her faith and sense of humor.

. . . We are grateful for the unselfish need — prayers of missionaries in South America where political situations are unstable.

Father, we are deeply thankful for your sustaining care, for your inspiration to our hopes. Remind us daily that honest prayers, offered in the spirit of love, have a powerful effect upon our lives.

Transform us with that power as we consider anew these words:
THE LORD'S PRAYER

Offertory Sentences
Isaiah 40:10

Offertory Prayer
Lord, grant us the insight to be half as generous with our pocket-books as you are with your grace. Amen

The Prayer Before the Homily
Your voice is as clear today as when you spoke to Eve and Adam. When you speak to us personally, we experience prayer. When you speak to us collectively, that is preaching. Through his humble servant, move your people to committed action. Amen

The Dismissal/Benediction
"After you have suffered a little while, the God of all grace, who has called you to his eternal glory in Christ . . . To him be the dominion for ever and ever. Amen" (1 Peter 5:10-11)

15. CHRISTIAN WITNESS

Invocation
Spirit of the living God, we know that you are with us at all times. The church throughout the centuries has sustained itself with that awareness. We sense your assurance of salvation this very moment. Thus, quicken us to transmit that spiritual wholeness to others who are broken. Amen

The Prayer of Confession
Our eternal Galilean, as you walked among our ancestors, you knew their loneliness and rejection. You told them that the luxury of affluence and religious respectability was silence. That statement alone sealed your death warrant. Could it be that spiritual renewal and church growth is minimized by our failure to speak out? We confess that our intentions are good, but that does not always give positive results.

Please deliver us from our mastery of indecisiveness and from the delusion that we can effectively share your truth only if the occasion is convenient. Grant that our vision will be wide enough to be receptive to those small signals — often disguised as struggling needs. Help us to recall that, by staying awake, others will see that we have something vital for them. Amen

The Prayer of Intercession
Lord, recently a great deal about honesty and humanness has been transmitted your way. But sometimes we can become too human, to a point where we tolerate impatience and anger as legitimate graces. Most distressingly, we feel that stands in the way of an effective church witness. There is a great hunger on our planet for love and acceptance. People do not expect truth — communicators to be perfect — just compassionate and caring. Help us to be one-third open, but two-thirds supportive.

Lord, we see that your message can be conveyed through a million channels. We ask that you will intervene:

. . . For a mother who is anxious over her son's moral destructiveness and wants to reach out with your love, but, at the same time, doesn't want to turn him off. *Encourage her with the hope that love can be demonstrated more effectively than spoken.*

... For industrial employess who produce inferior products and appear late for work — and wonder why the unemployment rate is so high. *Awaken them to the reality that no nation is greater than its apathy.*

... For evangelists who appeal to moral weakness with fear and sympathy. *Give them an awareness that honesty and love are necessary steps for spiritual growth.*

Appeal now to our strength in your authentic language of prayer: THE LORD'S PRAYER

Offertory Sentences
Hebrews 6:10

Offertory Prayer
Father, acknowledging that you accept a pure heart more than any offering we can bring, in these presentations, open the channels of our faith so your love will flow freely to others. Amen

The Prayer Before the Homily
In our task of reconciliation and healing, caution us of placing statistical reports before human beings. Spare us of playing the odds with passing half-truths.Sensitize us with a truth that changes people and their cultures. Amen

The Dismissal/Benediction
Leader: You have heard the sound of his trumpet.
People: The foundations of our lives have been shaken by his truth.
Unison: We have been called to a ministry of reconciliation. We enter the world to share our talents. Our strength will be our love. Amen

16. VISION AND CHALLENGE

Invocation

Lord, if we climbed the highest mountain in search of the deepest answers to our uncertainties, would you be there? And if we deciphered the molecular mystery of the snowflake, would you, also, be there? Today, amid our searchings and struggles, let us discover, anew, the vitality of your presence. Amen

The Prayer of Confession

Lord, there is a longing in our hearts to ascend to the stratospheres of your joy and peace. We have reached for you through the vaulted ceilings of our sanctuaries — but often our praise rebounds as a hollow echo. We have tried to communicate with you through the rich expressions of stained glass — but, like a cold cloudy day, the light of our feelings has not come through. We dazzle our minds with eloquent sermons and our hearts with fugues and hallelujah choruses — but, on Monday morning, return to business as usual.

Lord, we want to get through — to touch, to know, to love, and to 'be.' We seek to be reborn with new challenges and opportunities. With your hammer of forgiveness, come, and smash those chains which have imprisoned our flowering potentials. Come, and liberate us to a world where truth sharpens our senses to sterling beauty and where commitment outlasts cardboard philosophies. Amen

The Prayer of Intercession

We want to be made like a rainbow, Father. We see an inner being which can be flooded with a vast spray of colors. Then as a mirror of faith, we may reflect the beauty of your goodness outwardly. Father, send forth your mellow greens of truth to dispel our deceptive thoughts. Shower your gentle, caring blues to wash away our loneliness; your vibrant yellows of peace to scatter our impatience.

Within the beauty of this moment and with hearts grasping for your wonder, let us not forget the needs of our neighbors. Reflect, we pray, your multicolored love to those who merely exist on the dark and grey fringes of suffering.

. . . For refugees and boat people whose dream for a sanctuary in America is dashed by closed ports. Keep their dreams alive. *Protect them in your care. Give them a purpose for which to live.*

. . . For our president who must override partisanism in order to see clearly the best interests of our country. *Remind him that he has prayerful support in the difficult decisions he must make.*

. . . For countries with the resourcefulness to aim for the stars as a solution to their energy problems. *Enable us to work together for peaceful goals instead of struggling over destructive ends.*

Focus now your Spirit into the inner space of our hearts as we pray:
THE LORD'S PRAYER

Offertory Sentences
Matthew 6:33

Offertory Prayer
You have set the stars in the night sky. You have joined heaven and earth with your rainbow. You came yourself with the greatest gift, LOVE. May we remember that you alone are the Source of our strength as we share these expressions of devotion. Amen

The Prayer Before the Homily
Remind us, O Lord, that preaching becomes just another academic question until it is articulated in love. Amen

The Dismissal/Benediction
Our Father, the hour which we experienced challenged us to use all our time, energies, and resources to achieve your kingdom. You have given us challenges, not solutions. Help us to be explorers of truth, seekers of justice, compassionate human beings in a world bent on exploitation. Amen

17. STEWARDSHIP

Invocation
Master Creator, who has delegated us as human beings to be caretakers of this planet, enable us to see that responsibility translates into participation . . . time . . . talents . . . money. Amen

The Prayer of Confession
Father, we pride ourselves in being names to church and community committees, but neglect to invest the necessary resources for completing the job. We strike for more leisure time, but do not know what to do with the hours we already have on our hands. We are frustrated by time traps and hectic paces, but fail to realize that it is we who make the schedules in the first place. We advise our friends with the words, "Better late than never," but do not pause long enough to say to a stranger, "I care!"

Help us, Father, to unwind our tangled lifestyles. In that way we can set our schedules in step with your cosmic clock. As we shorten our wasted hours, so lengthen our opportunities to serve you more efficiently. Amen

The Prayer of Intercession
Father, a coin exchanges many hands in the process of conducting business. But to what extent do we allow ourselves to be spent in improving human relationships? You have planted us here to accomplish something important. We have a role to play in your divine enterprise. You have given us a unique gift. No one else will be able to make that contribution for us.

The life you have created for us, Father, is long on beauty, but short on time. In our locked-in smallness it becomes easy to avoid responsibilities and waste precious opportunities. Please remind us, at various points, that investments in people become our most enduring contributions. Sensitize us to the joys of those possibilities as we pray:

. . . For youth, bored by TV, who turn to video games for excitement. *Reveal to them other creative outlets, such as reading a good book.*

. . . For church members who will spend $150 for a new dress on Saturday and give you $5 on Sunday — and feel they have done you a favor. *Show them their potential for growth through giving.*

... For highway patrol persons who give of themselves patiently in order to save the lives of motorists. *Empower us with the truth that an ounce of prevention is worth a pound of cure.*

Instill within each of us the true spirit of giving as we preview Jesus' formula for a healthful economy:
THE LORD'S PRAYER

Offertory Sentences
Romans 6:20

Offertory Prayer
We ask, dear Lord, that we will match these gifts with a generous heart and a sympathetic concern for the poor and disadvantaged. Amen

The Prayer Before the Homily
Father, your Word discloses that preaching is good-news-giving. Together, they make kingdom building achievable. Now, so deliver unto us your Word that even our pocketbooks will say 'Amen.'

The Dismissal/Benediction
Lord, we are a community of givers, not takers. Through our daily relationships and business transactions, encourage us to share that truth. Amen

18. CHRISTIAN MATURITY

Invocation

Our Good Shepherd, may we uncover the truth that grace does not always come suddenly but, like the growth of a tree, gradually and consistently. Amen

The Prayer of Confession

We present the pages of our lives as a closed book. They have not remained open to the refreshing winds of renewal and the exciting possibilities for growth. Our paper-thin faith is torn by our pretense to be more mature than we really are. Playing this game of make-believe discipleship creates stress and sleepless nights. There is a point where pretending ends and fact-revealing about ourselves begins. Direct us to that point.

Lord, deal mercifully with our misguided motivations. We want to conform our thought patterns after your perfect love. Make us weak enough to submit to your grace and strong enough to commit ourselves unselfishly. Amen

The Prayer of Intercession

Lord, we are thankful you have made us as simple as a flowering tree. You have filled us with your strength. We can feel it as it flows upward through our frame. It is a warm, sustaining, presence.

You have made us strong. Your life-giving, life-sustaining strength has given us power — power to be free for growth and happiness, power to live harmoniously with others, power to grow and to pursue a life of unlimited possibilities.

As we affirm your power within us, we are also aware of people without power, in our society and in our world. Convey, we ask, your judgment and grace to those persons in positions of power who forget the powerless.

. . . Professional athletes who have arisen out of destitution and made it big with a six figure salary . . . but have forgotten the poverty of friends who helped them. *Make them mindful of their responsibilities to persons who befriended them.*

. . . County commissioners who evade key issues by resorting to legal jargon and name-calling. *Blind them with the facts that lasting progress comes through patience — and plenty of it.*

. . . Our system of government which sent youth to fight in Vietnam and tolerated their return without dignity. *Reach out to them, not only with helpful words but with opportunities for employment — and to prove themselves as useful citizens.*

Lord, deliver us from shallow formulas and overnight short-cuts to a mature and fulfilling life. Empower us with your catalyst for growth as we pray:
THE LORD'S PRAYER

Offertory Sentences
John 15:4

Offertory Prayer
In the measurement of spiritual maturity are not the deeds more effective then the testimony or argument? Enable us to inch forward in that discipline with the sharing of these offerings. Amen

The Prayer Before the Homily
We pretend to be an age of answers. Yet, if war is less attainable and hunger more unbearable, then how far have we come, morally? Grant us the honesty to wrestle with the question, "What is truth?" Amen

The Dismissal/Benediction
Leader: Why have you come to worship in this gathering place? Why is it so unusual?
People: We have come to deepen our faith and broaden our perception.
Leader: Can you be more specific?
People: We have encountered a love which will mature our talents and render us coping ability in the face of problems. Amen

19. THE CHRISTIAN HOME

Invocation

Lord, with the warmth of your illuminating presence, enter the house of our private selves. Come to scatter the dark mists of fear; come to disperse the webs of apathy. Amen

The Prayer of Confession

We keep on trying, Father. We make some headway here and grow a little there. But then we again sink deeper into our quagmire of self-centeredness. We are receptive and easy to live with only if it is convenient, only if it serves our purpose at the moment. Marital separations and family feuds often appear to be the rule rather than the exception. In our homes we have not achieved unity with diversity, but anxiety without honesty.

Our Father, we, your children, are homesick for peaceful stability. Come and adopt us anew. Reabsorb us into your family fellowship. We want to experience the transforming touch of your love, while our children are still with us. Amen

The Prayer of Intercession

O God of the human family, our Father of love, our Forgiving Son, our Caring Mother, the Comforting Spirit, we, your children, gather under the shadow of your umbrella for renewal. We bring before you our prayers, each one infinitely important, because it speaks to real persons . . . your unique creation. You established the human family for a purpose. Not only is it the cornerstone of our society, but it provides the tools wherewith the highest form of happiness may be secured. We thank you for that gift. We thank you for the gift of each other.

We summon your Spirit with its power to forgive and to renew, on behalf of others. There are those in the human family who have failed to be participants in your generous gifts:

. . . Parents, whose violent behavior deprives their children of the possibilities of a peaceful world. *May they grasp the truth that unless peace is practical at home, it will be impossible elsewhere.*

. . . Students, who juggle courses, desperately attempting to discover their major purpose in life. *Fill their intellectual emptiness with your supportive truth.*

Create a new sense of friendship in each of our homes as we share in your words:
THE LORD'S PRAYER

Offertory Sentences
Ephesians 6:8

Offertory Prayer
Our children are a priceless gift, Father. We desire that they will experience life in its fullest. It is our prayer they will discover today that gifts, given in love, will always return as friendships and blessings. Amen

The Prayer Before the Homily
O timeless Shepherd, with your Word, do not shelter us against the harsh pressures of the world; instead, empower us to face them courageously. Amen

The Dismissal/Benediction
O God, you have spoken in the language of truth. We have responded with joy. Now, your church family scatters itself among the brokenness of the world. Embrace us with your Spirit as we face that task. Amen

20. MOTHER'S DAY

Invocation
Our Lord and Father, whose love we have known through the warm embrace of our mothers, enfold us again in your care and acceptance. Make us strong in our fellowship sharing today. Amen

The Prayer of Confession
Father, they have given us the best of themselves — the gift of life. Yet, we confess that, unintentionally, we have accepted the daily efforts of our mothers as the norm. Rarely do we take the time to say, "Thank you." Too frequently we find ourselves saying, "Mother will always be there when we need her." Worse still, with our staggered schedules, we have denied her opportunities for creative expression. How long has it been since we gave her the day off? Father, please pardon our insensitivity to identify with their moments of doubt and frustration. As they wooed us with infant lullabies, so tenderize our hearts with your gentle calling. Calm our restlessness with your peace. Amen

The Prayer of Intercession
Our Father, the dove is one of the most beautiful creatures in your created order. When the great flood receded, your servant sent forth that 'grace on wings.' It reclaimed a twig of new life.
It was a symbol that peace had been made between heaven and earth.
The rainbow celebrated that union.
That dove reminds us of the beauty of our mothers.
Their white appearance . . . purity of intention in the molding of our character;
the soft feathers . . . their gentle touch before bedtime;
the cooing voice . . . their peaceful assurance during illness.
We know that our mothers are human. Like each of us, they stand in need of your encouraging grace. Father, be understanding:
. . . To mothers who must carry the cross of an alcoholic husband. *Lay before them the truth that persons must be loved for who they are — not what they are.*
. . . To mothers who must raise their children without a husband. *Challenge them to seek supportive acceptance from a Christian*

48

Alanon group.

. . . To mothers who confine their lives to afternoon 'soaps' and garden parties. *Lead them to personal fulfillment as a volunteer in the hospital or another community service.*

Lead each of us toward spiritual purpose as we renew ourselves in the words our mothers have prayed:
THE LORD'S PRAYER

Offertory Sentences
John 14:12-13

Offertory Prayer
Kind Father, we cherish this moment as we commemorate persons who have given us so much of themselves. May we continue to achieve their strength as we impart our love with these gifts. Amen

The Prayer Before the Homily
Our Father, help us to be receptive to your Word of truth as we are open to our mothers' words of wisdom. Amen

The Dismissal/Benediction
Our Lord and God, we rejoice that the T.L.C. or tender loving care of our mothers has been rekindled. The memory and influence of that strength will never leave us. We pray that you will remain with us, too. Amen

21. PENTECOST

Invocation
Your Spirit is empowering, Father. At creation it moved with light upon the face of the waters. At Pentecost it moved with power upon the face of the disciples. With our faith uplifted, move upon and within us now! Amen

The Prayer of Confession
Our generation is preoccupied with power, Lord, the power to exploit, the power to change, the power to annihilate. Why, then, do we run and hide when your power is ignited in our midst? Are we so fearful of encountering intimacy in our relationships — perhaps even unlocking our potential for growth? The glitter of the 'palace of things' has dimmed our vision of your sanctuary of values. As a result, we have conceived your flaming Spirit as nothing less than a prodigal phantom, lost in the past of our faith.

O Lord of acceptance, deal mercifully with our feelings. Our ache for spiritual rebirth has not been met. From the abundance of your amazing grace, cleanse us afresh. Uplift us with your power. Claim us for renewal. Let it begin now . . . today! Amen

The Prayer of Intercession
O Christ of faith, the Creator of pentecostal happenings and the Sustainer of all lasting renewal, why are we so impatient with your generous gifts? The sun continues to rise every morning. The rain is sent to refresh the ground. Food is on our tables at mealtimes. Why should our confidence be any less regarding the descent of your Spirit into the reservoir of our needs? When we consider all the dimensions of your goodness, we wonder why we have become so hesitant in sharing your spiritual growth potential with others. Your Spirit can change the world as Pentecost One demonstrated. Its power has as much potential for change today as it did centuries ago. The only difference is the attitude and the altitude of our faith.

Meet us, O Lord, in the vicinity of our need. Stand near to us so that we may see clearly the real truth about your Spirit. In that effort we intervene:

. . . For those who attempt to confine your healing power to the instantaneous laying on of hands — and play down your gradual healing process. *Etch into their minds that most of your healing is accomplished through the day-by-day prayers of many.*

. . . For those who gladly receive the gift of your Spirit, but neglect to cultivate its disciplined fruits within your church. *Establish an awareness that the joys of descipleship begin with giving and sharing.*

. . . For those who leave churches over petty doctrinal issues, spend millions for new church facilities, while millions of stomachs remain empty. *Guide them to clear thinking as to what is most important.*

Encourage us to recommit ourselves to the unity of your spirit — regardless of our denominational affiliation — as we pray:
THE LORD'S PRAYER

Offertory Sentences
1 Peter 4:10

Offertory Prayer
In response to the stirrings of your Spirit, the disciples spoke in the tongues of praise. For your unsearchable blessings, we lift our gifts in grateful praise. Amen

The Prayer Before the Homily
Send now your Word on the wings of your wind. Fill our deflated hopes. Mend our brokenness. Amen

The Dismissal/Benediction
"May the God of peace himself make you entirely pure and devoted to God; and may your spirit and soul and body be kept strong and blameless until our Lord Jesus Christ comes back again." (1 Thessalonians 5:23, paraphrased)

22. CHRISTIAN MARRIAGE

Invocation
Lord, as with a marriage relationship, covenants are made to endure. As we enter this convenant of praise and worship, may our relationships become more permanent through your love. Amen

The Prayer of Confession
We acknowledge, Father, that successful marriages do not *happen*. They require honesty and velvet communications. We must work and work at them. We also confess that our 'failure factor' is high. There is our problem of pride which consistently stands in the way of tender relationships. It clogs up our capacity for listening; it toughens our insensitivity and weakens our potential for trust.

As the Peacemaker of nations, come to us in our marriages, and calm our tension. Come not to mend, but to heal our brokenness. Remind us to dream again . . . together! Amen

The Prayer of Intercession
Lord, this prayer is about leading actors and actresses of the human drama . . .husbands and wives . . . ourselves. We have won few Oscars as directors of marital success stories. There seems to be fewer of them lately. There are the isolated singles with children, the Hagars and the Ishmaels who desperately search for acceptance in a family-oriented society. There are the betrayers of truth — and ultimately of each other — the Samsons and Delilahs who discover all too late that they've lost their most priceless possession: each other.

Please bend your ear our way, Lord. We appeal on behalf of those of us who have difficulty in getting our marital act together . . .

Couples who have been married for less than five years, and who have not begun to master the art of compromise. *While they're still young, bend their pride so they will see that peace is never made in an armed camp of hostility.*

Couples who have been married for nearly twenty years. Their romance is scarcely alive. A good time together consists of a night out with friends. They are lost by themselves. *Inspire them to work and work again for a lasting intimacy.*

Couples who have been married for nearly thirty years. Their children have families of their own. Now, they have very little to live for. *Lord, deliver them from their fearful aloneness with each other. Salvage their useless hours together in volunteer work wherever their interests and abilities are needed.*

Reveal now the possibilities of continual marital growth as we expose ourselves to your Son's words:
THE LORD'S PRAYER

Offertory Sentences
1 Corinthians 15:58

Offertory Prayer
Lord Jesus Christ, accept us with our failures, our hopes, and our possibilities. May these gifts become a means whereby we may touch the unacceptable and the unloved. Amen

The Prayer Before the Homily
We are grateful, O Lord, for the new possibilities your Word creates. Many of our marriages need that renewing quality today. Amen

The Dismissal/Benediction
Leader: If you could summarize Christian marriage into one word, what would that word be?
People: Commitment!
Leader: Love bears all things, believes all things, hopes all things, endures all things. (1 Corinthians 13:7)
People: God is with us. He will direct our ways. Amen

23. THE HOLY SPIRIT

Invocation
Our Forever-Emerging Spirit, disclose anew the potential for your Spirit in our lives. May we never journey far from your caring presence. Amen

The Prayer of Confession
Again, we drift comfortably before you. Living independently from those who really need us, we felt we could 'go it alone' without your help. But we were wrong. We have returned to rediscover our purpose for living and our possibilities for living. We have returned to recapture your timeless way: the power of acceptance and pardon.

We return to you, Father, because there is no other hopeful Presence available. We return to you because we yearn for food to live and light for the journey. We simply want to be free. Thank you for being here when we needed you. Amen

The Prayer of Intercession
Your Spirit moves in mysterious ways, Father. It can miraculously transform the human mind and heart. Accept our gratitude for its movement into our simple daily affairs — the care-free laughter we experience during holidays, the freedom to be ourselves in home sharing groups, the diplomacy of peace which, thus far, has prevented a nuclear holocaust.

We are grateful also for your concern for those who have separated themselves from an active participation in your spiritual gifts:

. . . Those who are indifferent to church growth opportunities. *Remind them that we need one another's support more than ever.*

. . . Those who consistently get their own way in church planning — even at the expense of others. *Open them to the joys of peace of mind which comes from taking an occasional backseat.*

. . . Those who take pleasure in twisted gossip and violent B-rated movies. *Confront them with the question, "Will you leave the world better than you found it?"*

Ignite us, we ask, as we recall to mind the eternal words of renewal:
THE LORD'S PRAYER

Offertory Sentences
Luke 11:13

Offertory Prayer
We sacrifice these gifts, dear Lord, in response to your continual blessings. Receive also our renewal commitment to serve you more closely day by day. Amen

The Prayer Before the Homily
Father, your Spirit winged its way to Jesus at his baptism; your Spirit spoke to the infant church through the flaming power of Pentecost; now, it addresses us through the voice of your servant. Amen

The Dismissal/Benediction
Lord, your mind drifted our way and played its familiar song. We affirm, "You were here!" But we must also ask, "Will we be there, too?" May our faith respond decisively as we journey again into the world. Amen

24. FATHER'S DAY

Invocation
Our Father in heaven, who has carried us safely through the shadows of night and who has introduced us to the possibilities of a new day, calm our fears. Guide our thoughts to the inner sanctuary of your truth. Amen

The Prayer of Confession
Lord, we are reminded of Solomon's wisdom, "The just man walks in his integrity: his children are blessed after him." (Paraphrase of Proverbs 20:7) Doesn't that mean that many of the problems of our children can be attributed to our near-sightedness?

Father, forgive us for not being honest. We have failed to uphold the high standards we have required from our children. Father, forgive us for being so caught up in the narrowness of our jobs that we dismiss the depth of family intimacy.

Lord, grant us the humility to accept your forgiveness and the wisdom to learn from our mistakes, so that honest 'fathering' can take place. Amen

The Prayer of Intercession
Our Father, we experience you best as the head of our family. Your courage to love us, in spite of what the world thinks, gives us an acceptance that will not quit. Your patience in forgiving us is really quite revolutionary. Your generous sprinkling of stars and snowflakes brightens our aloneness; and we recognize that we are never alone. We feel fortunate to be recipients of your generosity. Our problem is we can become so caught up in our immediate needs that we forget greater humankind.

Release us from that obsession as we petition on behalf:

Of fathers who are unemployed, with a son or daughter in college. *May their family strengths keep them going.*

. . . Of fathers whose jobs have deprived them of precious time with their families. *Provide them with opportunities when the quality of time together will render lasting security.*

. . . Of fathers who cannot openly communicate with their children, but whose 'always there' presence speaks louder than words. *Thank you for their grace to listen without complaint.*

Father, please accept each of us within the warmth of your presence as we pray:
THE LORD'S PRAYER

Offertory Sentences
Deuteronomy 16:17

Offertory Prayer
Our heavenly Father, as we attempt to place our best foot forward in the presentation of these offerings, grant that the footsteps we leave behind will be large enough to follow. Amen

The Prayer Before the Homily
The Good News is acceptance. The prodigal son returned home because he had never forgotten that truth. We pray that we, as parents, will be as successful in implanting that Word in the hearts of our children. Amen

The Dismissal/Benediction
Our eternal Christ, as we leave your house of praise, help us as fathers to take more initiative in conducting family devotions and growth experiences. May we as a family also cooperate in that venture. Amen

25. TRINITY SUNDAY

Invocation
All-knowing Father, who loved us through your Son and who nurtured us through the witness of your Spirit, journey to us, anew. Tranquilize our inner selves with your peace. Prepare us to meet the challenges of the coming days. Amen

The Prayer of Confession
O God of a hundred names, yet the Lord of one love, we confess our reluctance to acknowledge you as such. Our schedules of dull routine have spun us into circles of boredom. Our affairs with pleasure fads have diverted our attention solely to ourselves. Our journeys into the dark caverns of pessimism have kept us out of touch with your consistent acceptance. Our word games have sewn us into the "I" and "Me" pockets of greed.

O God, for our failure to respond decisively to your call of obedience and accountability, we beg forgiveness. Put us in touch with your sure-footed promises. Renew us with the cleansing balm of your grace. Amen

The Prayer of Intercession
O Lord of the "kingdom and the power," through the thunderclouds and the flashing lightning, we know that you are still there . . . and here. Even though your laws of nature can bring us disaster — we know that your law of love is greater than life itself. Your consistency in caring never diminishes. While nations are leveled and forgotten, your truth will stand.

It is with our confidence in your continual, outpouring Spirit that we reach forth to meet real human needs.

. . . The need for a successful land developer who, out of pride, places buildings before marriage and children. *In his excursion downward may he find happiness only after he acknowledges you as Lord.*

. . . The need for an elderly couple whose meager pension forces them to live on pet food at the end of the month. *Battle our apathy until we become involved in the hurts of a society that's becoming increasingly older.*

. . . The need for an upper middle class mother who replenishes

58

her boredom with "uppers" and her insomnia with "downers." *Allow her to see her authentic 'self' through the hungry eyes of her children.*

Deliver us from our papier mâché 'selves' as we rediscover Jesus' words:
THE LORD'S PRAYER

Offertory Sentences
Proverbs 22:9

Offertory Prayer
With the words of the Psalmist, we discover you as our eternal Father. Within a manger on a cold night, we discovered you as the Redeeming Son. With the flaming Presence at Pentecost, we discovered you as our Comforter. Now, may we become givers through these offerings — and discover you more personally in our lives. Amen

The Prayer Before the Homily
O Indwelling Spirit, illuminate our entire being. With your changeless message, seek out our hidden talents. Expose us to possibility living. Amen

The Dismissal/Benediction
"May God give peace to you, my Christian brothers, and love, with faith from God the Father and the Lord Jesus Christ. May God's grace and blessing be upon all who sincerely love our Lord Jesus Christ." (Paraphrase of Ephesians 6:23-24)

26. CHRISTIAN VOCATIONS

Invocation
Lord Jesus, who has given us minds to think with and hands with which to work, in these moments of reflection, remind us that we, also, have hearts with which to feel and to believe. Amen

The Prayer of Confession
Father, more frequently than we are willing to admit, we feel that our lives are misguided. By our own choosing we have taken an exodus from the truth about ourselves — and what we are capable of becoming. Our lives are like dormant seeds in ancient tombs, cut off from growth-bearing light, the illumination of your love. As Americans we affirm, "Life, liberty, and the pursuit of happiness." But whose life? Free for what? Happiness for whom?

Father, forgive us for affirming slogans which sound good, but ring without value. With your light of multicolored possiblities, focus upon our gifts. Remove our dark shadows of doubt so that we may really see. Amen

The Prayer of Intercession
O God of darkhorse prophets and Cinderella saints, the transformer of tree surgeons from Tekoa and tentmakers from Tarsus, with your arm of acceptance, reach down to our level. We are indecisive, impatient, befuddled as to where we should go. But you know where we ought to go. We come to you today out of our concern for persons without a dream.

. . . Children so influenced by TV that they want to grow up to be anti-heroes instead of advocates of humane causes. *Teach them the lesson that the achievement of mature happiness is a by-product of open hands, not a closed pocketbook.*

. . . Youth who want to give themselves to a vocation that outlasts life itself but are caught in the web of hard facts: inflation and job scarcity. *Encourage them with the hope that your will for them transcends economic trends and statistical probabilities.*

. . . Young adults who, during the sixties, opposed the war and middle-class hypocrisy, but who have forgotten their dream of 'selling out' to the system. *Summon their hearts and minds to the words from "The Sounds of Silence."*

Turn our hearts to the rhythm of the language of the Lord's prayer:
THE LORD'S PRAYER

Offertory Sentences
2 Corinthians 9:7

Offertory Prayer
We covet the privilege, our Father, of contributing to your grand enterprise; and, indirectly, to the shaping of morality in the lives of others. Amen

The Prayer Before the Homily
Each of us were created with unique gifts and talents. Our faith is capable of transforming them into a fulfilling vocation. In response to your challenge, enable us, as John Wesley suggested, "To earn all we can, save all we can, and give all we can." Amen

The Dismissal/Benediction
Leader: God has made known his intentions to you. Have you been listening?
People: Yes, and we are grateful for the gifts he has entrusted in us.
Leader: But how will you know that your abilities are his gifts?
People: "For God is at work within you, helping you to want to obey him . . . " (Paraphrase of Philippians 2:13)

27. STUDENT RECOGNITION SUNDAY

Invocation

We confess that we have permitted secular attractions to cloud the vision of your presence. Claim our individual attention, dear Lord, that the focus of our heart's eye will be on you — and you alone. Amen

The Prayer of Confession

Leader: From a cold-steel hopelessness which arrives early and over-stays its welcome; from a pious love which smiles but rarely touches;
People: Lord, have mercy upon us.
Leader: From houses that pretend to be homes; from abusing parents who have no guilt;
People: Lord, hear our prayer.
Leader: From self-serving political clout which grinds under the needs of children with learning disabilities and retarded adults;
People: Lord Jesus, deliver us.
Leader: From words without feeling, feeling without thought, and thought without mystery;
People: Lord, sustain us with the grace to be human. Amen

The Prayer of Intercession

Lord of white wool and black coal, of red sunsets and blue ber-ries, we celebrate your creative uniqueness within us and your star-spangled vastness about us. We come to you from where we are. We come as youth of a transitional society, deeply involved in the process of seeking, discovering, learning. Our requests are few, Lord, but they are honest ones:

. . . Please keep the flowers growing. Their beauty is a reminder of what our institutions should become with the right kind of tender loving care.

. . . Allow your pure mountain streams to keep flowing. Their mes-sage is clear — all purity and goodness flows into the reservoir of human generosity.

. . . Send us occasional eye-dazzling rainbows. Without them, panoramic splendors would be reduced to video games.

Lord, we are asking that you will remember people, too. Like us, our friends are weak, but they are the only ones we have.

... A nurse and a medical student on the brink of graduation: *Propose the question, "How are you going to lessen the moral pain in your world?"*

... Advocates of nuclear disarmament. *Ask of them, "Do your non-violent actions at home match your ideological pacificism?"*

... Youth and adults who are so hooked into religious cults that they are incapable of getting out on their own. *The horrors of Jonestown are still before us, Lord, would you ... could we ... allow that to happen again?*

Keep our motives pure and our actions on target as we pray together:
THE LORD'S PRAYER

Offertory Sentences
1 Corinthians 7:7

Offertory Prayer
Lord of history and the twentieth century, who has given us this beautiful planet called earth, accept these tokens of our deep gratitude ... and in that way we can help mold tomorrow, now! Amen

The Prayer Before the Homily
For the taste of freshly buttered popcorn on a November evening, for friends who stand by us when we are down, for energy that flows through our veins, for parents we have difficulty in understanding but love anyway, for your truth which sets limits on our moral freedoms, we give you thanks. Amen

The Dismissal/Benediction
Lord, we, as youth, have seen the spiritual void in our generation. It has created suffering and boredom. As we enter again into our world, challenge us with your fulfilling truth. Give us enough hope to live successfully one day at a time — yet not expecting all our problems to be resolved overnight. Amen

28. WORLD HUNGER

Invocation
With hungry hearts we seek the cool waters of your peace. With your
word of truth, however, stir those waters. As we worship freely, may
we remember that there are those who have no choice but hunger
and starvation. Amen

The Prayer of Confession
　　Our life-sustaining Father, there are too many color TV's and too
few playgrounds for bored children; too many well-funded political
campaigns and too few advocates of children's rights; too many laws
with tax loopholes for the rich and too few jobs-with-dignity for the
unemployed; too many street people and too few churches who will
sacrifice one warm room for shelter; too much communion bread
for Christians who have had breakfast and too few cups of milk for
children who accept one meal a day as the norm.
　　Benevolent Father, do not remove the guilt from our tables on
a planet of scarcity. Through the mystery of your grace, forgive us
. . . but continue to judge our insensitivity to hunger issues. May
our hunger after righteousness far outweigh our rich diets and extravagant clothing. Amen

The Prayer of Intercession
　　Eternal Father, we acknowledge you as the "fount of every blessing." In your biblical record we find your grace all too amazing. Your
ability to pull bread out of nowhere leaves us in awe. Moses received
tons of manna over a forty-year period. The ravens fed an exiled Ezek-
iel. The angels dined with your Son following his wilderness temptation. Father, there is a question to which we cannot find an answer.
"Are not the empty stomachs of the Third World any less deserv-
ing?" Who is their Moses? What angels minister to them?
　　Our Father, who broke bread for the redemption of humankind,
we who live in our smug and private world too often take your Son's
words, "The poor will always be with us" at half value. We fail to
understand his broader mandate, "Feed my sheep." Today, we want
to take that command seriously. It is our prayer that others will take
it seriously, too.
　　. . . We pray for those who export grain, not to feed the hungry

64

but to fatten livestock for the rich in those countries. "Let justice roll down like waters, and righteousness like an everflowing stream." (Amos 5:24)

... We pray for overweight church executives and leaders, who organize committees and give eloquent speeches on world hunger.

... Give your bodies to God. Let them be a living sacrifice, holy — the kind he can accept. (Paraphrase of Romans 12:1)

... We pray for a Pakistanian family of five who have only one loaf of bread to last for three days. "I am the bread of life, he who comes to me shall not hunger . . . " (John 6:35)

Accept our prayer of intercession, Father, as we pray in the spirit of him who said:
THE LORD'S PRAYER

Offertory Sentences
2 Corinthians 8:9

Offertory Prayer
Within the security of these walls, we lift these gifts in grateful praise. There are others who do not live under a secure roof. We ask that, through these resources, life will be made tolerable for the two-thirds of our global family who must go to bed hungry every night. Amen

The Prayer Before the Homily
Lord, we have enough food to feed the world. If the poor of the Third World would acknowledge your hand as the source of their food, then your dream for a peace on earth would heighten. May your Word now open us to the possibility. Amen

The Dismissal/Benediction
Father, we have hungered after righteousness and you have filled us. As we depart with satisfied hearts, continue to stir us to "feed your global sheep." Amen

29. SOIL CONSERVATION SUNDAY

Invocation
Our Creator, we are thankful for the natural beauty of this day. Your love for us is as consistent as the sunrise. We celebrate your blessings of health, fresh air, and caring friends. Amen

The Prayer of Confession
We are afraid for our planet, dear Lord. We are fearful of ourselves, of the monster of greed we have created with our technological hands. Like a computer Frankenstein, will we let it grow out of control and dominate us? We confess that we have prohibited your Gospel from touching the bedrock of our existence — Mother Earth. We have been thoughtless in polluting our resources of water and air. Can this madness continue forever? Have we considered what condition our environment will be in if we continue to litter our roadsides with aluminum cans, if we continue to clear forests without replanting?

Lord, shatter our illusion that blue skies and green trees will forever be guaranteed. Sensitize us to see conditions as they are. Cultivate in us the courage to change our lifestyle. Amen

The Prayer of Intercession
O Lord of crystal lakes and July rainbows, we are woven inseparately within the fabric of your good earth. You have created our bodies out of sixty percent water. Why, then, do we contaminate your rivers and oceans? The oxygen for our lungs comes from the air. Why would we want to poison it? Our food supply is extracted from the topsoil of your planet. Why should we expose it to erosion and deforesting? We are making progress in that clean-up effort. But it hasn't been easy. The exploiters of your planet continue to move on their collision course with self-destruction. We want to help them to reverse their pace.

. . . We want to help grandparents who fail to recycle their newspapers and aluminum cans, and who make no effort to contribute to community clean-up campaigns. *Remind them that every 'litter bit' can affect and alter the environment of their grandchildren.*

. . . We want to help campers and hikers who deface our national forests and game refuges. *Help them realize there will be no sanctuaries if these are destroyed.*

. . . We want to help oil companies who deliberately mix waste toxic chemicals in fuel oils. *Judge them with your tough love that they may change their destructive course.*

Help us to cultivate a heaven on earth as we are reminded of our responsibilities:
THE LORD'S PRAYER

Offertory Sentences
Acts 10:4

Offertory Prayer
Our Maker and Redeemer, you have given us the land with which to plant, till, and harvest. We have labored in appreciation of that gift. We now return a portion of it to you. We trust it will yield a harvest of peace and goodwill. Amen

The Prayer Before the Homily
Like the change from winter into spring, your Gospel addresses the cold winter of our souls, but never without the promise of the spring of hope. Amen

The Dismissal/Benediction
Leader: ". . . Glorify him for his mighty works." (Paraphrase of Job 36:24)
People: "Everyone has seen these things from a distance." (Paraphrase of Job 36:25)
Unison: "We feel his presence in the thunder." (Paraphrase of Job 36:33)

30. CREATION

Invocation

Out of the earth's darkness, you gave us light. Out of the darkness of a brutal society, you gave us the light of your Son. Out of the darkness of our sins, illuminate us with the light of your acceptance. Amen

The Prayer of Confession

We say honesty is the best policy. Many of us believe that it's okay as long as it applies to others. But how honest are we about the following question, "When was the last time we paused to witness a sunset in concert?" Did we say, "Hey, that's nice," and hurry on? Why didn't we praise your goodness in it?

Why do we live as if our lives were thrown together by some cosmic accident? Does that suggest that we have dismissed you as Creator and Sustainer? If not, why do we increase our chances for a nuclear holocaust with our sophisticated arsenals?

Like the dew of an early summer morning, descend upon us. Dispel our arrogance. Humble us until we acknowledge you as *Lord.* Sustain us with your life-giving energies. Amen

The Prayer of Intercession

Our Creator and God, long before you touched our blistered planet with your cooling rains, and who has recorded in your mega-galactic mind every amoeba that has ever lived, you had a design for our lives. Your love for each of us was far greater than the world itself. You fabricated each of us as miniature images of yourself. You formed us to dwell in harmonious relationship with this planet. When that occurs, all systems work smoothly. Why do some people dismiss that possibility in their behavior?

. . . We are disturbed by those who seek to genetically alter the human fetus, to create a master race through cloning.

. . . We are disturbed by local school boards who purchase books on creation which omit your biblical account. *Caution them that without your order in the universe, we would have been outdone by our craftiness long ago.*

. . . We are disturbed by politicians who, in purchasing tools of war, extract health care from children and the elderly.

Grant us fulfillment in your creation as we absorb ourselves into your Son's words:
THE LORD'S PRAYER

Offertory Sentences

With the eyes you have created for us, we witness a January moon, splashing the terrain with its silver splendor, or a blade of grass, saluting an April rainbow. With a million other marvels they awaken us to the intricate tenderness of your care. Stir us with that sensation of wonder as we participate in this offering experience. Amen

The Prayer Before the Homily

Our eyes gaze unto the hills from which comes our help. Our hearts are transfixed on the pulpit from whence comes your Word, the source of our light and life. Amen

The Dismissal/Benediction

Father, we know that you ask no more of us than to go forth as a committed people. Challenge us to put teeth into that through our clean-up efforts in this global village called Planet Earth. Amen

31. CHRISTIAN DISCIPLESHIP

Invocation
Our Father in heaven, you come to us through the man, Jesus, to teach us the way, the truth, and the life. Out of love you identified with us and accepted us. We rejoice. Inspire us now to demonstrate the joy and power of that love in our gathering today. Amen

The Prayer of Confession
Father, we talk about the 'harvest of souls' in our church meetings, but have neglected to cultivate the fruits of your Spirit in our lives. Our hands of *love* are clenched with anxiety; our *joy* has soured; we seek world *peace* only on our own terms; our *patience* has regressed into a tattered virtue; *kindness* is a nicety we exchange as a thoughtless custom; *goodness* is a seasonal Thanksgiving basket; the absence of *self-control* is reduced to a courage power failure.

May your Gospel of salvation touch us where we hurt, where we love, where we hope. When that happens, we can respond to your compassion with an Isaiah-patterned assurance, "Here, Lord, send me!" Amen

The Prayer of Intercession
Lord, like James and John, we see this stranger moving up the beach toward us. His pace is brisk and steady. The closer he comes, the more deliberate his presence. His eyes elicit our individual attention. Now, he is stopping. He says, "I am Jesus, the Christ. Come, follow me!"

Lord, that magnetic personality really is no stranger. You walk among each of us today. You come with the decisive words, "Join with me now. You may never have this opportunity again." You move among the lepers of Calcutta, the lame in Lamberene, the hungry in Haiti, the $50,000 career single, the mother who has lost her infant son, the unemployed textile worker, the inmate in prison.

Lord, for those who have been deaf and blind to your coming, we offer our prayer of intercession.

... For those who have allowed their educational achievements to complicate their faith to the point of frustrated, highly critical doubt. *Challenge them to blend common sense into their faith enrichment.*

. . . For those who wrestle with the insoluble questions as, "Why must the good die young?" *Sustain them with the hope that everything, even suffering, has a distinct function in your divine plan.*

. . . For church members who cheat customers in their businesses, acquire a stomach full of ulcers, and wonder why their 'Sunday only' religion had failed them. *Remind them that the price of discipleship is high — a complete commitment to your love.*

Lord, continue to feed our faith with your grace as we remember again these words:
THE LORD'S PRAYER

Offertory Sentences
James 2:17

Offertory Prayer
The Creator of all nations and the Father of us all, we dedicate these tithes and offerings. We trust they will be transformed into opportunities to extend your caring fellowship to others. Amen

The Prayer Before the Homily
Lord, you called Peter, James, and John out of the water. Similarly, summon and surround each of us with living waters as we participate in your message of hope. Amen

The Dismissal/Benediction
". . . God who gives you hope will keep you happy and full of peace as you believe in him." (Paraphrase of Romans 15:13) Amen

32. THE CHURCH

Invocation

In spite of our short-sighted faith, your grace has kept us together. We are grateful that, through our weakness, you have demonstrated to us the lesson of undying hope. So keep us humble in our witness of love, that we may wear the feet of peace and the hands of compassion. Amen

The Prayer of Confession

Our gracious Shepherd, who gave Peter the keys to your kingdom, forgive us for closing the doors on our one-dimensional church. Forgive us for pampering our buildings and omitting the wounded needs of friend and neighbor alike. Forgive us for avoiding the pain of the new birth of your Spirit which comes in ministry to and with others. Forgive us for living with the illusion that your kingdom will be established without our efforts.

Lord Jesus, we recognize that you have been more generous to us, your church, than we deserve. When we take the exodus to worldly respectability, you always leave the back door of your peace unlocked. More than a voice of conscience, may our purpose become a song of character and hope. Pour your baptismal waters over our troubled souls. Wash away the dark night of sin and apathy. Restore our unity. Amen

The Prayer of Intercession

Lord Jesus Christ, we are grateful for your breathing organism, the church. It is very much alive and on the move. Most vitally, Lord, we are thankful for the church's conscience — a sword of truth which slices through the sham of our times. We are thankful for her willingness to suffer for that conviction rather than compromise with the glittering half-truths of the evil one.

Certainly, Lord, your church has the potential to become an earth-moving, people-transforming force. With the enduring power of your grace, reach into the hearts of those who hold responsible positions in your church:

... The living dead who pave the road to spiritual inactivity with padded pews. *Rattle the window panes of their stained glass apathy with your trumpet of joyful good news.*

... Church board members and teachers who become frustrated by the lack of support received from their congregations. *Open to them new doors of inspiration so they may keep going.*

... Ministers who permit their theology to separate them from fellowship with other ministers — and the possibility for cooperative efforts with their churches. *As with Peter, say, "Feed my sheep."*

Sustain us, the church of the eighties, with a grace that breaks itself down into concrete commitment — one which echoes in these words:"

THE LORD'S PRAYER

Offertory Sentences
Exodus 35:21

Offertory Prayer
Lord, we do not arrive at the feet of your presence on our strength alone. We have been sent through the prayers of others — your caring community, the church. Stir us with a new sense of power as we distribute our resources in your name. Amen

The Prayer Before the Homily
In response to your Word, we, the people of the covenant community, your church, pause to rethink our mission. We thrive on hope and love, our vehicle for loving the unloved. Amen

The Dismissal/Benediction
Leader: There's nothing that can hold back the church.
People: We know when all else fails, the church's ministry of needs is always there.
Leader: Then go and continue to share the ministry of reconciliation. From his branch, blossom forth and grow.
People: We remain open to the winds of his Spirit. Amen

33. CHRISTIAN MORALITY

Invocation
Lord, there is a world of difference between an obligation to an institution and a responsibility to a suffering neighbor. As we confront you, remove our masks as a church and speak to the authentic 'us.' Amen

The Prayer of Confession
Why must life be complicated? Why has the pastoral scene of the Good Shepherd been transplanted by a more contemporary Cosmic Christ? There are too many decisions to be made. Worse still, they must be made quickly. There are too many decisions to be made about tomorrow. "Will they adversely affect the environment of our children?"

Father, please dismiss our failure to distinguish between being 'good' and acting 'moral.' Spare us from being manipulated by the issues which violate your truth. Instead, may we challenge them on every occasion. We desire to be our real selves for a change. Amen

The Prayer of Intercession
O God of Mosaic commandments and Galilean parables, you have sent the One whose love does not make our decisions any easier. Rather, he is the One who promises that, regardless of the outcome of our decisions, they can have a happy ending. Life is not necessarily a stage, but a gigantic mural where, day by day, the color tints of our decisons are painted.

Most of our portraits, O God, are not spared from the absolutes, the primary colors — but from an unpredictable mix of pale-grey hues. Please recognize that they are honest colors — they portray the real 'us' in all of our fumblings. Rarely do we produce a rainbow of moral perfection. But that's okay. Your expectations are no greater than what you have given us to work with.

Accept now our concerned prayer on behalf of those who must live out their lives daily on the fringes of the precarious greys.

. . . The brain surgeon who must inform a twenty-seven year old husband that his wife has a brain tumor — and only six months to live. *Help him/her to see that their honest compassion goes further than pretending to know the answers.*

. . . The sixteen year old who asks, "Why can't I do as I please with my body?" *Remind him or her of a further question, "Is getting pregnant — and being forced into parenthood too soon — a really cool form of freedom?"*

. . . The traffic violators who creep by stop signs and fudge on the opposite side of the road. *Please help them to lay to rest their hostilities before they are laid to rest permanently!*

Sustain us with a grace that begats a 24-K commitment as we pray together:

THE LORD'S PRAYER

Offertory Sentences
Psalm 50:14

Offertory Prayer
How fortunate we are, Lord Jesus, to participate in your unfolding drama of love. Help us to be committed, not only in our giving to your kingdom, but in our living before others, as well. Amen

The Prayer Before the Homily
Speak to us now through the voice of the prophet, but love us with the silent voice of compassion. Amen

The Dismissal/Benediction
Father, Thomas Edison once said that, "If we did all the things we are capable of, we would literally astound ourselves." As you sensitize us to human need, remind us that there are no limits to your love. Amen

34. HUMAN NEEDS

Invocation

Almighty God, to the ancients you dwelt in the secret place of the most high. Yet we know you dwell not beyond — but with us now. You have descended from your throne of grace to touch our hurts and to meet our needs. That is our prayer today. Amen

The Prayer of Confession

Eternal Eye of heaven, you see us. Beneath this frame of walking protoplasm you probe and find the 'withdrawing us' compromising with the tentacles of indecision . . . you find the fearful 'flinching us' struggling through the shadows of doubt . . . you find the 'shallow us' dieting on half-baked truth and sugary slogans.

Come, Eternal Eye of grace, expose our blindness so that we, too, may see ourselves as you see us . . . through the eyes of need-supplying love.

> Overpower our longing for community;
> Your presence is unmistakable;
> joy is abundant;
> peace prevails!
> Thank you!
> Amen

The Prayer of Intercession

Lord, I am a delicate mechanism within the human body. I am ultra sensitive — easily hurt when neglected. But I also respond with euphoric joy when I am congratulated. As a rose petal, I am so delicate — yet so human and alive. I think you created me for a special purpose — without which life could not be hopeful. I am a person's need.

Recently, I have become difficult to live with. I do not reveal myself as clearly, due to the increased stresses of today's world. My only hope is love, your love, which removes the layers of self-deception and group pressure. When our basic needs are unmet, Lord, anxiety and pain can set in. Consider, if you will, the frustrations of those who cry for acceptance.

. . . Elementary school teachers who are not always appreciated by parents of students and who are taken for granted by a permissive society. *Whisper comforting words of encouragement when they reach their daily lows.*

. . . Grandmothers who live miles from their grandchildren and are unable to see them but once a year. *May they find at least partial acceptance through occasional phone calls and letters.*

. . . Lawyers who can benefit financially from a tax loophole, but realize to do so would mean their children could suffer with increased taxes. *Give them the wisdom to see that the health of a nation begins with honesty — not craftiness.*

Expose your love before all our needs as we participate together in these words:
THE LORD'S PRAYER

Offertory Sentences
Matthew 25:35

Offertory Prayer
As human beings, we express a personal need to be loved, to be recognized, to be accepted. Fulfill our need for acceptance as we give you these alms. Amen

The Prayer Before the Homily
You appeal to our minds with a liberating truth; you appeal to our untapped energies with justice; now appeal to our needs with your accepting love. Amen

The Dismissal/Benediction
You have encountered, perhaps, life's greatest moment. Your needs have been exposed to the Master Designer of human dignity. Submit yourselves daily to that Source. Turn your needs Son-ward. Amen

35. EVANGELISM

Invocation
As we become participants of the Light of the world — and seek to impart it to others, Father, help us to distinguish between *being* good and *doing* good. Amen

The Prayer of Confession
Your servant, Jonah, seemed to have his act together. No one questioned his sincerity. He understood your Law and loved it. Yet he overestimated your strategy for Ninevah. You called his hand and he rebelled. Are we any different when we lock ourselves into far-sighted goals and second-rate strategies for Gospel-telling? We're homebodies with a freeze-dried theology. But, for all of us, the Great Fish of justice awaits.

Father, the ringing and throbbing chorus of your Gospel falls on minds dulled by TV reruns. Having misplaced our telescope of faith, we no longer aim for the stars. Plunge us now into the pounding surf of your forgiveness. Cleanse our vapid hearts with the thrill of your ageless message. Fill us afresh with your living waters. Amen

The Prayer of Intercession
Lord, evangelism could be defined as giving ourselves until our pockets are empty — and still feeling rich at the same time. We have responded to your mandate to become givers of good promises — not takers in a disposable society. We do not delight in being spectators in cold storage. For a while, it can become a comfortable feeling . . . no risks/no hits/no runs/no errors. We say, "Let God accomplish his own work. We are so human and error prone. After all, God is God."

It should be the urgency of your Gospel which is the wind at our backs. It is that holistic, all-inclusive power which throws us into the arena of violence, hunger, and suffering. We, the fellowship of your power, seek to participate more deliberately in that struggle. Please grant us the courage to ask the right questions about who we are and where we should be.

. . . Why do overweight church leaders sit down at an $8.00 steak dinner and complain about the loss of church membership? *Prick their complacency until they reshuffle their priorities and get back in tune with where the people are.*

. . . Why must ministers confine evangelism to a fall revival and a padded church roll book? *Broaden their perception with a Gospel that supplies basic human needs.*

. . . Why is it, as Carlysle Marney once suggested, that every church that's alive is on the edge of heresy? *Jar loose the cobwebs of congregations that they may share in the wedding feast of renewal.*

Keep our hopes alive as we move forward to the rhythm of these words:

THE LORD'S PRAYER

Offertory Sentences
2 Corinthians 8:12

Offertory Prayer
Our Father, grant that our desire to share your message of redeeming love will be comparable to these first-fruit offerings which we present. Amen

The Prayer Before the Homily
There is a great yearning in our land for a rebirth of justice. History has demonstrated that the cradle of justice is truth. Lord, reawaken us to that exciting venture in this event called preaching. Amen

The Dismissal/Benediction
". . . So that the name of our Lord Jesus may be glorified in you, and you in him, according to the grace of our God and the Lord Jesus Christ." (2 Thessalonians 1:12)

36. THE CHRISTIAN HOME

Invocation
We do not come asking to be made perfect; neither do we antici-
pate that our faith pilgrimage will be easier. Simply, as your family,
empower us to be more effective builders of your kingdom. Amen

The Prayer of Confession
God, our Father, we have become so overwhelmed by the forces
of evil that we have closed our minds to truth and hardened our
hearts against justice. That insensitivity has even touched our family
relationships. Fetal children are aborted for the sake of convenience.
First-offender youth are imprisoned with convicted murderers and
drug pushers. Grandparents are taken to convalescent homes and
forgotten.

Father, in our suave dealings and manipulations, we discover
that we have come up short. We had hoped that our technology
would have delivered us a society void of pain and responsibility.
It has not worked out that way. Neither has guilt worked its way from
our consciences.

Extend your hand of forgiveness to us. Absorb our shock waves
of anxiety toward the future. Calm our restlessness. Bend our con-
victions back into your straight paths. Amen

The Prayer of Intercession
O God, our Rock of Ages, whose Son is the Chief Cornerstone
of our faith, come to reinforce our fragile life rafts, our homes. With
your ageless stability, unify our relationships as we struggle against
the 'white water' rapids of a secular culture. We thank you, not only
for the swirling eddies of change, but the gentle, clear streams of
holiday celebrations. We are beginning to see that all of these flowing experiences contribute to our fulfillment as persons and happiness as families. Our struggles have been difficult, but the joy far
outweighs the difficulties.

In humility we summon the outpouring compassion of your love
on families everywhere.

. . . To parents of children with leukemia whose long illness is
wiping out their life savings. *Send forth not only showers of blessings but generous contributions from our pocketbooks.*

. . . To parents whose sloppy life-style reflects to their children that it's okay to throw gum wrappers from their cars and leave half their food uneaten at supper. *Spray their conscience with the fact that polluted water may be bequeathed to their grandchildren as a result of their carelessness.*

. . . To newly married couples who approach their relationship as a disposable TV dinner. *Open the floodgates of your love that they may experience your lasting springs of joy.*

Teach us to "bear all things, believe all things, and hope all things" as we affirm as a family your Son's challenge:
THE LORD'S PRAYER

Offertory Sentences
Acts 20:35

Offertory Prayer
Help us to demonstrate by these gifts that even though the darkness of inflation may dampen the present, it is your promise of truth which will claim the future. Amen

The Prayer Before the Homily
Your Word, like a diamond, has many facets. Come to us like the tenderness of a child's touch, as firm as a father's discipline, and as open as a mother's arms. Amen

The Dismissal/Benediction
Leader: You are taking with you the hope of the world, the survival kit called the home.
People: We are seeing that, without God's guidelines for happiness — the home — the world will continue on its collision course.

37. YOUTH SUNDAY

Invocation

Heavenly Father, we are here for many reasons. We ask that this will become a period where we may gauge our ability to listen . . . with feeling. Amen

The Prayer of Confession

Our Eternal Galilean, your eyes bear down upon us again. They burn and etch their power upon our soul; we smoulder in guilt and shame. They seem to say to us, "Why didn't you love me? Am I that difficult to follow? Are my teachings out of touch with your needs?" But we cannot answer in honesty. Like Peter, we deny you and cannot explain why . . . that really hurts us. We promise we will try harder the next time, but when the next time comes, and the frenzy of temptation is upon us, like aimless tumbleweeds, we are carried by the winds of conventionalism.

Lord, there are those penetrating eyes again. We cannot evade them — we do not want to evade them. They are so caring and understanding. Come, assure us of your acceptance. Forgive us with a touch of grace so that we may resist . . . overcome . . . grow. Amen

The Prayer of Intercession

O timeless Galilean, you were forever young. Life came alive for you at every turn. You were the mender of broken dreams. Your path was on the cutting edge of history. Almost overnight you collected a band of visionaries in their early twenties. Many laughed, but your singular challenge, "Come, follow me," has had more of a transforming effect upon history than any other factor. As with Philip and John Mark, today's youth bring to your attention a desire to be challenged. They eagerly seek to be released from the limitations of a permissive society. Their emerging spirit burns with a quest for truth. Lord, please understand their quest.

. . . Look favorably upon youth who participate in competitive school activities. *May they learn the lessons of courage in defeat and sportsmanship in victory.*

. . . Look with understanding upon youth who struggle for acceptance by their parents, but fail to secure it. To fill the void they compensate with drugs and alcohol. *Give them the ability to see that there is no future happiness in chemical addiction.*

... Look with compassion upon the best of our youth who are unemployed and have little hope to secure a college education. *Encourage them — through us — to keep on trying, because history's most successful suffered hardship and struggle.*

In all our strivings to remain young at heart, ignite us with the adventure of hope as we pray:
THE LORD'S PRAYER

Offertory Sentences
Mark 4:24

Offertory Prayer
Lord, it is in giving that we become less possessive about the present and more optimistic about the future. As with Jeremiah, may we become benefactors of the 'tomorrow' through the sharing of these offerings. Amen

The Prayer Before the Homily
Lord, Paul Tillich has said that, "The first duty of love is to listen." Open now our ears so that we may truly live. Amen

The Dismissal/Benediction
Lord, help us to retain our individuality, that special gift you have given each of us. We know the peer pressure of today's world is severe. Yet, with your love, we will continue to affirm that it's great to be alive in the late twentieth century. Amen

38. LABOR SUNDAY

Invocation

Within the shelter of your everlasting arms, we seek rest from our labors, a burst of positive energy for our minds, and a rebirth of love for our souls. Amen

The Prayer of Confession

Lord, we are weary from a long week's journey. We admit that we have made it tiring by our own selection. Our work attitude and labor ethics have drained our creative energies. We have worried over job security and envied the jobs of others. We have demonstrated little pride in our workmanship and company growth. We have kept one eye on the time clock and our mind's eye on the weekend.

Lord, pardon our greed and selfishness. Make us grateful for healthy minds and bodies with which to work. Remove us from a preoccupation with our own 'wants' and plant us where there are critical needs to be met. We cannot work or live apart from your love. We need you now! Amen

The Prayer of Intercession

Dear God, our Creator, there is no greater gift than the creative mind and the energetic hand. We thank you for that. We are grateful because, together, those gifts can create fulfillment and purpose in our lives. As you promised your children centuries ago, through faith you will bless our efforts and help us to prosper. O God, many of us find joy in our daily jobs; we petition on behalf of others who are finding their work efforts frustrating.

. . . Those who have grown bitter with their jobs, who feel they have been passed over unfairly in promotions. *Remind them to be thankful for the jobs they do have. May they also see that injustices will be atoned by your truth.*

. . . Those who work for corporations who pollute either our natural resources or the human mind. *Work in their consciences a passion for wholesome truth.*

. . . Those parents whose job dislocation has created emotional insecurity among their chldren. *Restore their sense of family unity with your reconciling love.*

Supply now our vocational needs as we labor to realize your Son's words:
THE LORD'S PRAYER

Offertory Sentences
1 Corinthians 3:14

Offertory Prayer
In the presentation of these gifts, the monetary dividends of our labors, may we pledge also to labor equally for peace and justice. Amen

The Prayer Before the Homily
If we think of the Gospel media only in terms of entertainment, then why did they have you executed? Lord, may this be a time for agonizing thinking and deep reflection over the issues that really matter. Amen

The Dismissal/Benediction
"And now may the God of peace, who brought again from the dead our Lord Jesus, equip you with all you need for doing his will." (Paraphrase of Hebrews 13:20-21a)

39. REFORMATION SUNDAY

Invocation
Lord, as a church, spare us of hiding behind our stained glass saints. Grant us the courage to emerge forth into your healing light. Cleanse and equip us for your task of reconciliation. Amen

The Prayer of Confession
The flames on your altar are rekindled, Father. Through the gentle fanning of the Spirit, they reach forth to consume the dead wood of our superficial rituals and dry theologies. Yet, in the coldness of our hearts and through the insensitivity of our feelings, we evade those flames. We run and hide behind our comfortable pews. The white fire of inner renewal and outward reforms are too radical for us to grasp. Cable TV has our number. Zombies we remain until you arrive to sweep us away from our catacombs of fear.

Will our faith take the risks and follow your torch of hope? Father, lead us sunward to the gentle breezes of your acceptance. Keep us receptive to that kind of change which enhances peace and unifies families. Amen

The Prayer of Intercession
Lord, what sort of church would we have if we took seriously Dwight L. Moody's words, "The world has yet to see what God can do through one man totally given to him." At least for a while, that took place with your followers — men and women who were fed by the tonic of your resurrection and whose sails were filled by the breath of your Holy Spirit. You came . . . the world saw . . . and you conquered through love. The unity of the first century church kept its power alive and progressive. Our divisions, our many denominations, hinder the release of your power into our lives and into the problems of the world.

Lord, as your body, it is our prayer that your church will get its act together.

. . . There is a need for increased spiritual interaction in our sharing groups. *Will we set aside petty differences of doctrine and go about your task of healing the world?*

. . . There is an increased need for discussions among our church laity on the hottest topic of our time: nuclear disarmament. *Lord, if we cannot get together over the issue of survival itself, where does that leave the hope we preach on Sundays?*

. . . In light of the energy crisis there is a need for churches in individual communities to pool their facilities and resources. *Otherwise, how is it possible for them to demonstrate intelligent stewardship to the world?*

Equip your church for the challenge of the eighties with these practical yet hopeful words:
THE LORD'S PRAYER

Offertory Sentences
Malachi 3:10

Offertory Prayer
Unexpectedly, as a mid-July thunderstorm, the refreshing winds of your Spirit come to purify the church. Cleanse anew our motives for ministry as we endeavor to strengthen your body with these resources. Amen

The Prayer Before the Homily
O God of the abundant Word, renew us, your church, with a vision to trust in the future, grace to love as if our lives counted on it, and the courage to get moving. Amen

The Dismissal/Benediction
Father, when we return to the world with its vast injustices, enable us to remember the greatness of your church. Let us remember the millions who are fed with its hand . . . the hospitals which are staffed and funded by conscientious Christians . . . our church colleges and universities which balance knowledge with truth. Lord, let us remember, and may we be thankful. Amen

40. CHRISTIAN EDUCATION SUNDAY

Invocation
Today's celebration is not a casual gathering of the ecclesiastical pink lemonade society. You have called us with a mandate 'to be.' We have listened and pondered . . . and have come. Prepare us to worship you with the best that we have: a willing heart and an open mind. Amen

The Prayer of Confession
Lord of wisdom and truth, our trek toward full maturity has made little headway. We keep struggling and hoping, but somehow we end up where we started. We confess our frequent failure to think through the issues that really matter. We allow our computer to do our thinking for us. We have made low marks in our knowledge of church and biblical history. We continue to sit back and do little. We regulate our children's TV time, but offer little encouragement to study the Book of Books. Each Sunday, while the 'greatest story ever told' is enacted in our church classrooms, some of us go to sleep. What is wrong? Where have we failed? Is it too late to amend our ways?

Apply now your cleansing power upon our failures. Sweep aside our apathy. Restore our confidence in your truth so that we may have greater confidence in ourselves. Amen

The Prayer of Intercession
Lord God, whose Gospel is a graceful blend of truth and knowledge, we praise you for that unique apparatus called the mind. We are grateful for its potential for discovery, growth, and human progress. Recently, however, that has been academic. Why do we spend millions of dollars to elect public officials to serve us, but, among themselves, they continue to play "The Insanity Game" with nuclear arsenal build-up. Lord, if we lose our heads in that pastime, then we may not have heads at all.

Lord, we believe that you will not allow your planet to be detroyed before its time; but that does not mean that wars will cease. Please listen to our serious petition as we pray:

. . . For all church colleges and universities who attempt to communicate a principle of truth and justice in an age consumed by its short-sightedness. *Thank you for their courage and may they receive greater financial gifts from churches who complain about our deteriorating world.*

... For local school board members who make decisions affecting the knowledge development of children without public hearings. *Recall to them that they were elected by the people to serve the people.*

... For parents and teachers who argue over the issues of sex education and prayer in public schools, yet who spend less time acting on the global issues that really matter. *Teach them the vital truth that debate is never a substitute for action.*

Above all, instruct each of us to become effective ambassadors of your Gospel as we secure wisdom from these lines:
THE LORD'S PRAYER

Offertory Sentences
Psalm 92:1-2

Offertory Prayer
In your honor, O Lord, we share these gifts to be used for specific ministries. In this way, may our children learn that caring does not happen by chance — but by inspired leg work. Amen

The Prayer Before the Homily
How are men to call upon him in whom they have not believed? And how are they to believe in him of whom they have never heard? And how are they to hear without a preacher?" (Romans 10:14) (R.S.V.)

The Dismissal/Benediction
Leader: Return now to your homes and places of business as spiritually renewed persons.
People: Should we not also return as torchbearers of truth?
Leader: Yes, the world today is reluctant to invest wisdom and sanity into its peacemaking efforts.
People: "I am the light of the world. So if you follow me, you won't be stumbling through the darkness, for living light will flood your path." (Paraphrase of John 8:12) Amen

41. WORLD COMMUNION SUNDAY

Invocation
Lord Jesus, with enflamed hope we share in your Bread of Life. It is our desire that this table will become a launching pad from which we may feed the lonely and the abused. Amen

The Prayer of Confession
Lord, as we break this Living Bread, we remember the brokenness of our world family. We remember our mothers who slave to prepare wholesome meals for their families, yet who feel unappreciated. We remember our medical missionaries who give their lives to the task of eradicating disease and sin, yet become discouraged when prospering home churches send only quarters. We remember our youth, whose judgment and health are impaired by angel dust and the between class six-pack.

O Bread of Heaven, enter our brokenness. Heal our wounded feelings. Refill our dry lakes of doubt. Give us a new song of joy. Amen

The Prayer of Intercession
Lord, come and dwell at the head of our table. As we eat and fellowship together, loosen us from the petty anxieties of the day. In a spirit of relaxation and openness, come to laugh and rejoice with us. Make us grateful to be alive. May our experience together be love-filled and power-filled. May we secure the happy assurance that you are present to uplift, to strengthen, to challenge.

In this celebration of joy, we acknowledge the sorrow and pain of others.

. . . We remember all Christians in prisons throughout the world. *Restore their self-dignity and a hope for freedom.*

. . . We remember the blind and the deaf. *Assure them that your inner healing light will follow.*

. . . We remember all drug refugees, youth runaways, and metropolitan 'street people.' *Touch their aloneness with a friend who really cares.*

We offer this prayer in honor of your love as displayed in these words:
THE LORD'S PRAYER

Offertory Sentences
Exodus 25:42

Offertory Prayer
The question, Lord, is not 'where' or 'when' we should follow you, but 'why.' In the exchange of these elements and in the oblation of these gifts, grant us the resolve to answer that decisive 'why.' Amen

The Prayer Before the Homily
Share in our sorrows and joys, O Bread of Heaven. Feed us so that we may secure strength for the journey ahead. Amen

The Dismissal/Benediction
Lord, we have been guests in your house today. We are grateful for your hospitality and warm acceptance. Now, may we go and invite others to your banquet of life. Amen

42. CHRISTIAN MISSIONS

Invocation
With the urgency of your task, you called Peter, James, and John. Instill within us today a renewed vision of that urgency — that you are the only Way, the Truth, and the Life. Amen

The Prayer of Confession
Our Father, when we enter into your presence, we sense your love about us, your acceptance of us. We realize that your love has other dimensions as well. Your love is so awe-inspiring that we cannot begin to contain it. Like a freshly picked flower, it must be given away.

We regret to confess, Father, that we have been selective in our love. Often we are tempted to love just part of the world — not all of it. For some of us, the world could well be flat . . . with our country the center of attention.

Your voice is calling us through the hunger of India, peasant exploitation in El Salvador, disease in Micronesia. We *hear,* but do not *listen.* To be true to your Gospel we *have* to listen.

Kind Father, forgive our narrow perception. Pardon our narrow-minded compassion. Stir our consciences until we take that first step: Meeting the needs of our Third World neighbors. Amen

The Prayer of Intercession
Our Father of all nations, who has come to us with one Gospel, help us not to retreat from the problems of the world. By no means is your Gospel introverted. It is not characterized by clenched fists, but by open hands. Jonah was a 'fists' man — at least, for awhile. Declaring truth with your name on it made it a different story. We do not share your Gospel on our terms. Your design for our lives far outweighs our limited expectations. We are near-sighted. You can see into eternity.

Today, it is our desire to prayerfully intervene for those who live on the fringes of near-sightedness:

. . . Parents who discourage their youth from becoming medical missionaries. *Encourage them to see that if their youth fail to address the unmet needs of the Third World, then the forces of violence will.*

... Christians who equate the missionary enterprise exclusively with preaching and teaching. *Impress upon them the conviction that your task of good news sharing often involves carrying the Bible in one hand and a loaf of bread in another.*

... Bible translators whose tireless energies are contributing to the distribution of your Word among all tribes and nations. *Sustain their efforts with spiritual fulfillment.*

Fire us to be vehicles of your truth as we are supplied with the fuel of your words:

THE LORD'S PRAYER

Offertory Sentences
Psalm 54:6

Offertory Prayer
Our Father, we have recognized that the Good News begins with the word 'go.' We trust it has taken on a sharing effort, as well. May we grow in that 'sharing grace' in this act of stewardship. Amen

The Prayer Before the Homily
Deliver us, Lord, from a Jonah complex, from confining your Gospel witness to glass cathedrals and TV offerings. Enable us to see where the people are coming from. Then the church may proceed with the conversion of the whole world. Amen

The Dismissal/Benediction
"Always be full of joy in the Lord . . . his peace will keep your thoughts and your hearts quiet and at rest as you trust in Christ Jesus." (Paraphrase of Philippians 4:4-7) Amen

43. LAITY DAY

Invocation

O God, our Father, who has given us the wisdom to seek you and the strength to serve you, infiltrate the depths of our being. Sustain us with your power for the long journey ahead. Amen

The Prayer of Confession

Lord, this hour marks a special time in the life of our church. We as laity enter into the ministry of proclamation. However, we feel unworthy to do so. In our faultfinding, we have denied ourselves the possibilities of friendship. In our pettiness, we have clouded major national issues with local gossip and name-calling. In our stinginess with money and time, we have allowed organized crime to fill the void of the lives of our restless youth. In our cowardice, we have hidden behind our stained glass image, instead of facing human suffering head-on.

As you journey toward us, please meet us half-way with your hand of forgiveness. Set our stumbling feet again on holy ground. Redirect our eyes upon your cross. Thrill us anew with your Gospel of reconciliation. Amen

The Prayer of Intercession

O God of burning bushes and descending doves, it is comforting to know that you've still got the whole world in your hands. In spite of an erratic economy and the depletion of many of our natural resources, most people are basically good. In fact, there has been no problem that we have not been able to solve. We are still in the business of spiritual mountain-moving. The resources are available. The opportunities for witnessing are there. It just takes that added ingredient of faith.

Prayer is a good beginning. In our intimate conversation with you, we express a concern for others . . . that through our spiritual energies, they will be motivated toward your cross.

. . . Transform those who are awaiting trial. *Through a prison ministry, give them hope to face, with courage, a pronounced future. Give their families assurance, too.*

. . . Transform those who are complacent in their large homes and successful jobs. *Stimulate their thinking with your exciting*

Gospel of truth.

. . . Transform those whose minor league gods of gossip have enslaved their reputations. *Speak your healing words by our lips.*

Transform our faith to deeper levels of commitment as we are challenged:
THE LORD'S PRAYER

Offertory Sentences
1 Timothy 1:5

Offertory Prayer
Our Eternal Light of the World, remind us that a generous heart is a grateful heart, and that love flows freely from those who do not allow their possessions to own them. Amen

The Prayer Before the Homily
Your Word is alive; breathing with joyous hope. Your truth has coping power. It prepares us for your task of healing and witness. Amen

The Dismissal/Benediction
Arise as men and women of conviction. Be filled with God's goodness. Challenge the world with the *light* of the world. Amen

44. ALCOHOL/DRUGS CONCERN SUNDAY

Invocation
We praise you for the precious gift of life. As we renew ourselves in your presence, enhance our self-image. Remind us to be our own person — never to be possessed by anyone or anything. Amen

The Prayer of Confession
You created us as beautiful people — from inside out. The ugliness of evil can tarnish . . . even destroy us. That dark force can motivate our fears to twist the truth about ourselves, to fire our jealousies with anger, to feed our insecurities with those chemical life-disintegration forces. Life is too beautiful to be destroyed by self-destructive and dead-end drugs. Pain, abused children, shattered marriages, splintered homes, lost jobs are not worth it. Lord, forgive us for being so naive, to be taken in by their smooth advertising charms. The "kiss of death" is a sly predator. Understand our weaknesses as we seek to affirm our strengths. Encourage us in failure. Amen

The Prayer of Intercession
Lord, your most priceless gift to us is ourselves. We come packaged together with miles of capillaries and muscles on a peculiar-looking frame. We are a mystery to ourselves. You have placed us here to find happiness and to manifest your kingdom in our living.

We take for granted that our brain cells and organs will never deteriorate. We even speed up the process through consumption of alcohol and other chemical additives. That is not the way to express our gratitude for your generosity.

We summon your wisdom to infiltrate the erratic behavior of our time. Lord, we are victims of conditions beyond our control. For people whose lives have been abused by those forces, we share our concern.

. . . Children who are physically and verbally abused by an alcoholic parent. *Encourage them to love their parents for their strengths and not be resentful of their weaknesses.*

. . . Persons who drive home each evening 'under the influence.' *Make them see how many lives they are jeopardizing.*

. . . Families living on the fringes of poverty because parents use food and clothing money for alcohol. *Appeal to their sense of reason to seek professional help before their entire family is destroyed.*

Sustain each of us with the courage to face all our problems in the spirit of your Son's words:
THE LORD'S PRAYER

Offertory Sentences
Matthew 19:21

Offertory Prayer
As you require that we present our bodies acceptable in your service, likewise, as we present these gifts, we trust they will help create a more wholesome society — void of chemical abuse. Amen

The Prayer Before the Homily
We program our hearts and minds, Lord, with your need-fulfilling Gospel. It is our prayer that we will not only be communicators of your truth, but living examples, as well. Amen

The Dismissal/Benediction
Leader: Your preparations are complete. Again, you face the world. You have sensed the stimulating challenge of commitment.
People: "God has not called us for uncleanness, but in holiness." (1 Thessalonians 4:7)
Leader: Unlike anything that you have experienced, God will make you really free.
People: "If you obey my teaching you are really my disciples . . . and the truth will make you free." (Paraphrase of John 8:31-32)

45. BIBLE SUNDAY

Invocation
From a frustration with six o'clock bad news omens; from the darkness of a moral confusion in which we struggle daily; from the coldness of insensitive people who feed on borrowed hopes; we enter your "gates of thanksgiving and your courts of praise." Welcome us now with your timeless love. Amen

The Prayer of Confession
Lord of eternal beginnings and consistent love, we thank you for your mirror of truth, the Scriptures. It is there we observe ourselves through a variety of rich personalities. Our difficulty arises when we look too closely — we see ourselves too closely. For example, we see ourselves as a disenchanted *Eve,* forever brooding over big mistakes; as a rebellious *Jacob,* resisting again and again your design for our lives; as a complaining *Moses,* attempting to excuse ourselves from crucial witnessing; as a stubborn *John Mark,* determined to get our way at any cost.

Lord, overlook our imperfections. Overwhelm us by your grace. Transform our failures into history lessons of faith where we may gain from our mistakes. Amen

The Prayer of Intercession
O God, who inspires us with new beginnings in Genesis and holds forth the promise of happy endings in Revelation, speak to us in your language of acceptance. We expose before you the inner closets of our sins and the misty cellars of our failings. We await anxiously the ventilating winds of your presence to flow our way. As you came to us on the wings of your Word, splash your grace upon the sensitive wounds of our Spirit. Reconcile and reunite our shattered spirits until joyful fulfillment is ours.

Your Word, O God, functions more effectively than any healing balm. It reminds us further of our commitment to others. The words of Martin Luther suggest that, "The Bible is alive; it has feet, it runs after me; it has hands, it lays hold of me." For those who, either through ignorance or arrogance, short-change the potential influence of your Word, we direct our prayerful energies:

... For teen-age women who must decide whether or not to abort a human fetus. (We reconcile that it is a decision which only they can make.) *Remind them that to 'take a life' might deny our age another Florence Nightingale or Thomas Edison.*

. . . For cynics and grouches who have failed to love both their neighbors and themselves. *Open them to the spiritual treasures of your kingdom within.*

. . . For employees who see thievery only in terms of money taken, not time extracted from their jobs. *Encourage them to see that stewardship touches all of life.*

Pour forth the power of your Word as we affirm:
THE LORD'S PRAYER

Offertory Sentences
Philippians 2:13

Offertory Prayer
Gracious Father, address us not as a prophet on paper, but as a Word that witnesses and speaks to us where we are most possessive — in our pocketbooks. Amen

The Prayer Before the Homily
Challenge us, Lord, to the deeper dimensions of your Gospel. To be effective, we must allow it to speak to our waiting hearts. May it become more than a book of rules; instead, like a transmitter, a total way of life. Amen

The Dismissal/Benediction
"I commit you to God, who is able to make you strong and steady in the Lord, just as the Gospel says, and just as I have told you." (Paraphrase of Romans 16:25-26)

46. PRAYER

Invocation
Our Father, we regret that we do not glide gracefully into your presence. Rather, our flight resembles a wobbly pelican, off course and lost. Lay claim to our restlessness. Renew our faith so that we may soar like the wings of an eagle. Amen

The Prayer of Confession
Father, how do we find you? How may we stay in touch? We believe that the communication of prayer is one vital way. Yet how effective are we in that approach? The obstacles of self-centeredness and pride, of impatience and shallow faith stand in the way.

As you radiate forth your mercy through forgiveness, grant us the perception to listen with both ears and heart. Amen

The Prayer of Intercession
Lord, we feel like a stereo with deteriorated earphones. We believe prayer can work, we can even hear an occasional "still small voice" coming through. But the sound isn't always too clear. There is the static of doubt which clouds our concentration.

Tune, we ask, the frequency of your presence our way. Focus your grace:

. . . On those of us who see prayer strictly as a welfare check and a Thanksgiving basket. *Instruct us with the truth that the most effective prayers are boomerangs in nature — the more we give, the more you give.*

. . . On those of us who see prayer as a video game where we try to outmaneuver your will to our advantage. *Zero in on our elementary understanding of prayer. Enable us to see that prayer-power flows freely only when we let loose of ourselves.*

. . . On those of us who see prayer as a convenient 'on-off' crisis button. *Tune us in to the exciting, continuous open-channel frequency of your presence.*

Continue to inspire each of us to deeper spiritual dimensions as we pattern ourselves after the following prayer 'ideal:'
THE LORD'S PRAYER

Offertory Sentences
Acts 10:4

Offertory Prayer
As with our prayers, we offer these monetary dividends in faith. We pray that they will challenge our extravagant style of living. Amen

The Prayer Before the Homily
Thank you, Father, for your ageless Word. It has spoken significantly to every age. May we have the common sense and patience to see *that* when we complain about our petty problems. Amen

The Dismissal/Benediction
Lord, we have journeyed inward past our self-willed personalities to the sanctuary of your peace. Your warm, divine light has returned us again to life's drama. Among others, we will know the joys of loving, caring, and sharing. Amen

47. THANKSGIVING SUNDAY

Invocation
The Giver of all good and perfect gifts, it is time again to recount our blessings. Before we become too grateful, remind us to keep our praise in perspective. As our first priority, may we never cease to care. Amen

The Prayer of Confession
We confess, bountiful Father, that there is enough food to feed the world. The problem is *us.* In our blind greed, we fail — oftentimes intentionally — to see the empty stomachs and protein-deficient bodies of the world's two-thirds hungry. As Christians, we are seeing that greed and gluttony create ingratitude. Father, deliver us from a grave of possessions without gratitude.

As we participate in this annual act of thanksgiving, please purge our insensitivity. Purify our intentions so our checkbooks will speak louder than Sunday school rhetoric. Restore our humanity so we may be givers once again. Amen

The Prayer of Intercession
Our Father, who asks for no special faith favors except an occasional 'thank you,' we are here to do just that.
... For our children's teachers who were not paid bonuses for miles of patience and tons of love;
... for medical technicians who have made progress in cancer research;
... for mothers whose thoughtful hand-prepared, freshly baked bread daily;
... for inner city crisis centers which rescued an older child from prostitution;
... for a new friendship which will outlast a new car;
... for guardian angels who pulled us through Charlie Brown situations in spite of our fumblings;
... for Scrooges who cleaned up their act and helped finance a poverty-cycle youth through college;
... for physicians who administered to pain without being thanked;
... for children who laughed at falling snow and saw only the good in others;

. . . for high-protein meals that saved at least one child from starvation;

. . . for those who responded to the crisis of injustices and did not organize a committee;

. . . for those, upon hearing of their terminal illness, thanked you for the love they had known and gave their remaining time as a volunteer in a convalescent home,
we are truly grateful.
THE LORD'S PRAYER

Offertory Sentences
Colossians 3:17

Offertory Prayer
We are thankful for the common sense to be good stewards of our resources. Also, we are thankful for the wisdom to be sensitive to the issues that really count. Amen

The Prayer Before the Homily
Dear Lord, for sermons that uplift and do not bounce; for children who cannot sit still but, miraculously, remember everything that has been said; for choirs which display an angelic patience even when the preaching is 'off,' we are truly thankful. Amen

The Dismissal/Benediction
Thank you, God, for the delicate mechanism of our world and the creative flow of energy which keeps life young. Grant that every creature, every life form, will vibrate with restoring purpose. May each of us experience rainbows and butterflies forever. Amen

48. THE FIRST SUNDAY IN ADVENT

Invocation
We open our eyes to the drama of the ages. Your light has emerged.
Sensitize our hopes with the familiar signs of your coming: a star,
the angelic chorus, and a peasant stable. Amen

The Prayer of Confession
Leader: Like a symphony of angels flung on chariots of light, your
joy to the world, your joy for the world flashes again before us. Your
twilight on the nativity message touches our hopes and dreams.
People: Are we adequately prepared to experience your light? If we
allow it to blind us, then we miss both the medium and the message, the joy of preparation, and the joy of achievement. With that
Light of the World, is our faith adequately prepared to touch the darkness of hunger, disease, drug abuse?
Leader: Lord of exploding, pulsating light, shatter our stained-glass
smugness which filters in only what we want to see.
People: Yes, Lord, recharge our weary fears with a courage that
stands erect under fire. Provide us not with a road map to a comfortable, predictable Christmas, but with a challenge to carve out
our own unique way. Amen

The Prayer of Intercession
Our Father, the Reformer of Scrooges, we come as a people of
expectancy. We make miracles happen because we believe broken
people can be recycled. We have confidence in your love as a
cementing force in reclaiming shattered lives. Why else would three
sages travel for months seeking a unique gift on the tail of a star?
Why else would tattered shepherds awaken on a cold winter evening and see your thing that had come to pass?
Lord, the radiancy of your star is no less dim today. The problem
has been our reluctance to share the light. Touch our apathy with
a new sense of wonder. Through our efforts, may we touch many
who would otherwise find the holidays as stars without light and
packages without gifts.
. . . Shopping-bag ladies whose only Christmas dinner will be a
discarded Big Mac in a trash can. *Give them a family to love and
to be loved by.*

. . . Alcoholics whose monotonous succession of drinks become additional excuses for evading their problem. *Meet them on the road to Bethlehem with a love that doesn't ask questions — one that just accepts.*

. . . Single parents who will miss sharing their Christmas with that 'someone special.' *Please identify with that need through a grace of hopeful tomorrows.*

Now, keep our expectations aglow as we pray:

THE LORD'S PRAYER

Offertory Sentences
Hebrews 6:10

Offertory Prayer
Lord, those who participated in your first nativity did not present unto you their second best. Grant that through the preparation for your coming, we will invest our best offerings and sacrifice. Amen

The Prayer Before the Homily
O Christ of Bethlehem, we bring to you our dead-end dreams and splintered hopes. In this witnessing moment, bring forth your star of truth. Amen

The Dismissal/Benediction
Leader: Light isn't for everyone. It cleanses and illuminates. Shadows scatter and evil cringes.

People: Light stimulates growth. As the Christ Child will grow up and mature, so may we.

Leader: Reach forth. Behold. Touch. Emerge.

People: His light is our hope. Amen

49. THE SECOND SUNDAY IN ADVENT

Invocation
Lord, there are those who call Christmas the mystery of the Incarnation. You, however, arrived on the scene to level the mountains of religiosity, to make faith simple, and love achievable. Why can't we understand that? Help us to accept the fact that we are accepted by your love. Amen

The Prayer of Confession
As your pageant of Advent unfolds, O God, we still find ourselves off-stage, attempting to program your mystery of love and to compromise with truth. In our effort to rediscover you, we resort to name-calling. We call you *Wonderful Counselor.* Why haven't we consulted your wisdom amid our economic problems? We call you *The Mighty God,* but confine your greatness to winter sunsets and Easter lilies. We call you *The Everlasting Father,* but do not acknowledge you imtimately as a personal Friend. We call you *The Prince of Peace.* Why have we entrusted our efforts for peace in nuclear arsenals?

May this season become a time where our thoughts are motivated by compassion as you have transformed us by forgiveness. Give us a new confidence as we light our days with your triumphant love. Amen

The Prayer of Intercession
Lord, our prayer explodes with this good news: You are going to comfort us, to overlook our mistakes, and to secure us with happiness. Like the beating of a throng of angel wings, we hear your great voice. It increases in intensity. It shouts that you are coming and that your way will be made straight.

... We see a great light. We sense a great power unlike any kind we have ever experienced. This time it consists of compassion and humility. Its transforming ingredient changes people and makes historical things happen. You even promise to watch carefully over us like a shepherd cares for his sheep. In your cosmic mind you have each of us numbered . . . and our infinite value is immeasurable!

Why would anyone be blind to the obvious light of your coming? For those who continue to stumble painfully through the darkness of evil, we offer our prayers.

. . . For the world's seventy percent poor who own only fifteen percent of its resources.

. . . For those who have stopped sending Christmas greetings due to increased postal rates.

. . . For adult singles whose aloneness is particularly devastating during this season traditionally set aside for families. *Replenish their emptiness with your gospel of friendship.*

Lord, heighten our Advent experience as we enrich ourselves in your words:
THE LORD'S PRAYER

Offertory Sentences
Hebrews 13:16

Offertory Prayer
Our Father of infinite love, whose heavens spilled forth the song of redeeming peace, infuse within us your unspeakable presence as we dedicate these gifts in your honor. Amen

The Prayer Before the Homily
The Light of Bethlehem keeps shining through. O Light of Truth, come even closer to us. Sustain us with a hope that will last far beyond December 25th! Amen

The Dismissal/Benediction
"And now — all glory to him who alone is God, who saves us through Jesus Christ our Lord; yes, splendor and majesty. All power and authority are his from the beginning . . ." (Paraphrase of Jude 1:24-25)

50. THE THIRD SUNDAY IN ADVENT

Invocation
History marches in cadence with the drumbeat of humane goals. Your Son convincingly carried people's lives into that current. As we move a week closer to the celebration of his Advent, cleanse us. In that way we will be fully prepared to accept him with an open heart. Amen

The Prayer of Confession
We have a clear view of Bethlehem, Lord. Already, we can feel its pulse. Our hearts burn with excitement. But we are not 'home safe' yet. Traveling can still be hazardous. The detour signs of hurried schedules and last minute shopping stand in our way. The one-way streets of anxiety and fatigue are a constant threat to our tranquility.

Lord, we are so anxious to get there. Please forgive our impatience. We are weary of the tangled schedules we have woven. Dismiss, we pray, our confusion. With the magnetic force of your love, draw us gently and claim us as your own. With your ageless truth, keep us honest in principle and open to the needs of any who may need a friend. Amen

The Prayer of Intercession
O Christ of Christmas present, forever emerging as the Force eclipsing the ghost of Christmas past, we inch even closer to your infant cradle. Your star has directed us to the Bethlehem of hope. The journey has been straight, filled with wonder, and our preparations have brought us upward to this point. Our fulfillment is nearly completed. We need only your sustaining presence to direct us the rest of the way.

O Christ, we are acutely aware of the circumstances which hinder the happiness and fulfillment of many:

. . . We pray for the hospitalized who will have to spend Christmas in an antiseptic room. *Reveal to them the beauty of Christmas through carols and visits from friends.*

. . . We pray for those who share in the witness of Christmas caroling in high crime areas. *Grant their "songs of the air" will soften the hearts of those most hardened.*

. . . We pray for those nations who continue to escalate their stock of nuclear arsenals. *Help them to see that the only road to peace is the way of diplomacy.*

O Christ, please understand each family with their struggling needs as we pray your prayer:
THE LORD'S PRAYER

Offertory Sentences
Psalm 96:7-9

Offertory Prayer
The miracle of your Advent to humankind is clearly before us. Let us recreate that miracle of giving in the presentation of these tokens of love. Amen

The Prayer Before the Homily
Lord, the bad news is that we have struggled on the barren plains of secularism, caught in the bitter winds of the evil one. The Good News is that there is a way out — through a child. Share now that timeless story with us . . . anew. Amen

The Dismissal/Benediction
Eternal Spirit, whose incarnate truth — like the Christmas Star — splashes forth from the heavens, send us forth with a renewed spirit. Quicken us to become peace*makers* instead of peace*breakers.* Amen

51. CHRISTMAS SUNDAY

Invocation
Lord, in this encounter with your incredible light, give us the humility of the shepherds, the diligence of the wise men, and the wonder of the citizens of Bethlehem. Amen

The Prayer of Confession
O Divine Christ Child, we have arrived. We have decorated our trees with the Bethlehem Star on top and our gifts at the bottom. That symbolizes our two highest hopes: gift-giving and star-gazing. Sometimes, we sense that isn't enough. Is that why we feel so depressed after Christmas? We think only of ourselves and our immediate family circle, and are deaf to the cries of a hungry world that knows no Christmas dinner. By looking too high at the star, we overlook our necessary confrontation with the cross — and its sacrificial demands.

O Holy Child of Bethlehem, renew us like children, recapturing the truth of your salvation event. Then, remold us as women and men, fully responsive to and responsible for the demands of peace in a rapidly unraveling world. Amen

The Prayer of Intercession
Lord, all roads have intersected at the door of the Bethlehem stable. Many preparations have been made: mistletoe hung, cookies baked, toys purchased but unassembled, each tree decorated uniquely by respective families. What about our preparations for you? Have we spent at least half as much time for you as we have for the secular preparations? We pause momentarily to thank you for your superlative gift: your gift of acceptance. We belong to you and to your church.

Lord, in our prayer, we remember persons who must live out their Christmas alone . . .

. . . We remember parents and students marooned in air terminals and bus stations. *Enable them to see that Christmas is not a place, but an experience. May their unique Christmas away from their families be memorable.*

. . . We remember abused children who have lost their self-esteem and who find no excitement in giving gifts. *Arouse in their tender*

minds the power of hope, which transcends the ignorance and vio-
lence of their planet.

. . . We remember older adults whose limited savings and monthly
pension checks fall short in giving them a reasonably enjoyable holiday. *Sustain them with pleasant memories of Christmases past and
gifts from their younger Christian neighbors.*

Lord, in this generous season we affirm your goodness in these
words:
THE LORD'S PRAYER

Offertory Sentences
Matthew 2:11

Offertory Prayer
Father, many of us approach this day with mixed expectations. We
come in joyous praise of your Incarnation, yet saddened by the
sufferings of our Third World neighbors. We pray that these presents
will convey that we care enough to match food with faith. Amen

The Prayer Before the Homily
We are as wise men who come to worship your Son, yet fail to commit ourselves to his cause of peace and justice. Empower us to leave,
not star-gazed, but truth-filled. Amen

The Dismissal/Benediction
Lord, we have presented unto you the gold of our possessions and
the fragrant incense of our fellowship. We now journey forward with
the light of Bethlehem to our backs and the promise of Easter hope
to our faces. Please dwell with us forever. Amen

52. EPIPHANY SUNDAY

Invocation
Lord, in this time of short days and long nights, we need to be reminded that the light of your Star is as brilliant as ever. We seek that presence in this worship experience. Amen

The Prayer of Confession
Father, there is still "A Song in the Air" — the memory of fluttering angel wings is still clear and the homeward footsteps of the wise men are fresh. Most importantly, the Star continues to emit its promise of hope. Will we retain that exalted Spirit during these days of "the bleak midwinter"? It is easy for us to let go . . . to forget the moving experiences of the Nativity. Your Way is clear. Why do we make it so difficult with our static marital relationships, with our insensitivity to the need-cries of our children?

Father, as the foot of your Star directed us to the manger of truth, we pray that the arms of your Star will lead us forward to the Jerusalem of new-life possibilities. We wish to share in your far-reaching message of reconciliation. Give us another opportunity to try again. Amen

The Prayer of Intercession
O God, who illuminates life with your boundless energy source called light, in some ways we are relieved Christmas is over. Some of us experience a letdown, even near-exhaustion. Now, we feel we can pause to reflect upon the real meaning of what we have experienced. We see that your light is the eternal flame of hope. That is why we have come to your light. With your illuminating presence, you flow through us and drive away the dark shadows of prejudice.

With your light as a lamp unto our feet, help us to reach into the darkness of others.

. . . Married couples whose empty relationship keeps each of them miserable. *Enlighten them with the truth that the dividends of a sound marriage result from the investment of openness and hard work.*

. . . High school teachers who go a second mile in an attempt to keep students from quitting school. *Enlighten them with the hope that their efforts will never be forgotten by their students* —

regardless of how indignant they may have been at the time.

. . . Government leaders who believe that tinkering with nuclear weaponry does increase chances of a global showdown, but want disarmament only on their own terms, that is, they wait for other nations to disarm first. *Enlighten them with the sober fact that if cooler heads do not prevail soon, there may be no heads later!*

Recall to our minds our continual responsibility to others as we pray:

THE LORD'S PRAYER

Offertory Sentences
James 1:17

Offertory Prayer
We rejoice, our Father, that your Star of light has not faded from our view. We trust these gifts of light will give hope to the lonely, light to the blind, and comfort to the victims of war. Amen

The Prayer Before the Homily
Out of darkness, out of despair, out of aloneness, our cry for light and truth emerges. Meet that need in the preaching of your Word. Amen

The Dismissal/Benediction
Whatever is true, whatever is honorable, whatever is just, whatever is pure, whatever is lovely, whatever is gracious, if there is any excellence, if there is anything worthy of praise, think about these things. (Philippians 4:8)